BELFAST
THE CITY AT A GLANCE

Royal Belfast Academical Institution
Known locally as Inst, this 181…
school by archit…
more than…
marks the …
College Squa…

University of …
Originally hous…
art and design fa…
accommodate 15…
25-51 York Street, …

St Anne's Cathedral
Thomas Drew's 1904 cathedral is spiked by a 54m stainless-steel 'spire of hope'. Ornate 1928 Creation mosaics by sisters Gertrude and Margaret Martin are interior highlights.
Donegall Street

MAC
Hackett Hall McKnight's 2012 arts complex is the city's most accomplished cultural draw.
See p025

Robinson & Cleaver Building
Although this famous department store closed in 1984, its name lives on in a 2013 café by architects McGonigle McGrath.
See p051

Samson and Goliath
These two Harland and Wolff gantry cranes are reminders of Belfast's shipyard boom. Now they assist with marine engineering.
See p010

City Hall
Hillary Clinton reopened Alfred Brumwell Thomas' 1906 City Hall in 2009. The landmark affords a patch of green in the centre of town.
See p014

INTRODUCTION
THE CHANGING FACE OF THE URBAN SCENE

Belfast is in the midst of an extraordinary metamorphosis. After decades of underinvestment, the city is welcoming an influx of millions of pounds, the creation of new quarters dotted with lively bars and restaurants, and high-calibre cultural hubs like the MAC (see p025). A once sparse diary is filling with festivals, and the arts scene is blossoming. Most importantly, sectarian violence has been largely extinguished, bar the odd flare-up, to make way for peace. For architecture devotees, Belfast is a bubbling laboratory. The centre, which can be easily traversed on foot, is a collision of high Victorian and Edwardian styles, clunky 1960s and progressive 21st-century buildings. A taxi-ride away lie mould-breakers such as the award-winning Falls Leisure Centre (see p092).

The average age of Belfast's residents is 36, making this one of Europe's most youthful urban environments. Led by homegrown entrepreneurs, locals are starting to reclaim their city, expunging the memory of barricaded streets and reversing the flood to the suburbs. This transformation is far from complete, though. Micro-businesses are flourishing but may never recapture the economic glories of 'Linenopolis', when Belfast supplied textiles and ships to the world in the 19th and 20th centuries. Bleak corners and political division still exist, but cutting through all this is the city's most alluring asset – its people, their hospitality and *craic*, the best route to understanding Belfast's complex past and bright future.

ESSENTIAL INFO
FACTS, FIGURES AND USEFUL ADDRESSES

TOURIST OFFICE
St Anne's Court
59 North Street
T 028 9023 1221
www.nitb.com

TRANSPORT
Airport transfer to city centre
Airport Express 600 buses run regularly between George Best Belfast City Airport and the Europa Buscentre. The journey takes between 15 and 20 minutes
www.translink.co.uk
Car hire
Avis
T 0844 544 6028
Taxis
Fona Cab
T 028 9033 3333
Value Cabs
T 028 9080 9080
Taxis cannot be hailed on the street
Tourist card
The Belfast Visitor Pass (one day, £6.50; two days, £10.50; three days, £14) grants unlimited travel on all Metro, NI Railways and Ulsterbus services within a designated zone, and includes special offers and discounts for various attractions, tours, restaurants and retailers
www.visit-belfast.com

EMERGENCY SERVICES
Emergencies
T 999

CONSULATE
US Consulate
Danesfort House
223 Stranmillis Road
T 028 9038 6100
belfast.usconsulate.gov

POSTAL SERVICES
Post office
12-16 Bridge Street
T 0845 722 3344
Shipping
DHL
Unit 2, Edgewater Road Industrial Estate
T 0844 248 0710

BOOKS
Belfast 400 edited by SJ Connolly (Liverpool University Press)
Modern Ulster Architecture edited by Karen Latimer (Ulster Architectural Heritage Society)

WEBSITES
Art
www.belfastgalleries.com
Newspaper
www.belfasttelegraph.co.uk

EVENTS
Belfast Festival
www.belfastfestival.com
Belfast Film Festival
www.belfastfilmfestival.org
HouseHold
www.householdbelfast.co.uk

COST OF LIVING
Taxi from George Best Belfast City Airport to city centre
£8
Cappuccino
£2.50
Packet of cigarettes
£7.50
Daily newspaper
£0.70
Bottle of champagne
£50

BELFAST

Population
281,000

Currency
Pound sterling

Telephone codes
UK: 44
Belfast: 028

Local time
GMT

Flight time
London: 1 hour 20 minutes

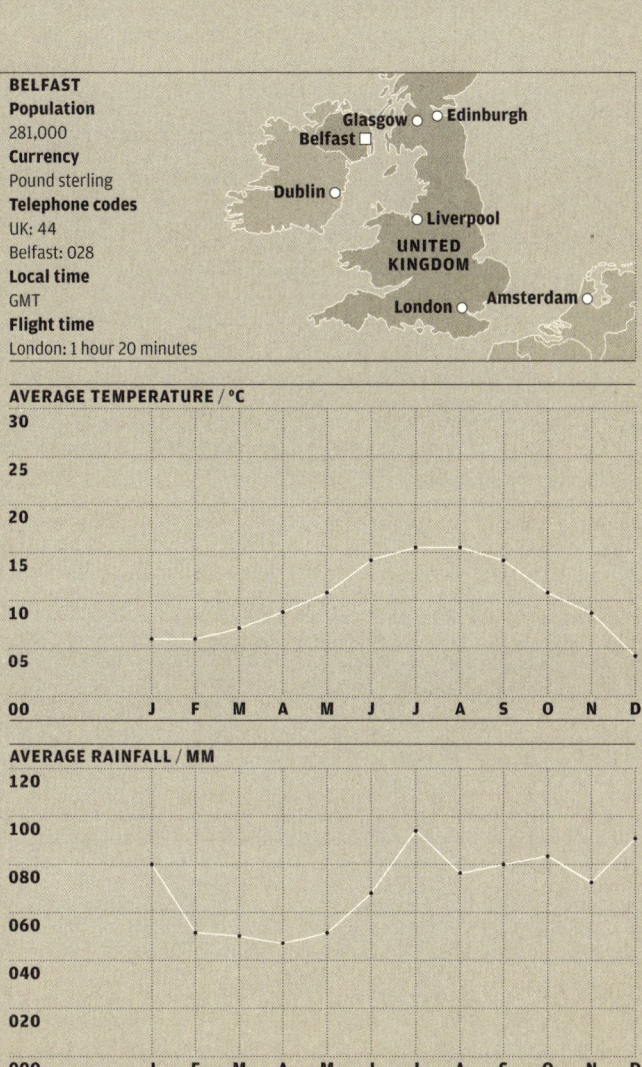

AVERAGE TEMPERATURE / °C

AVERAGE RAINFALL / MM

NEIGHBOURHOODS
THE AREAS YOU NEED TO KNOW AND WHY

To help you navigate the city, we've chosen the most interesting districts (see below and the map inside the back cover) and colour-coded our featured venues, according to their location; those venues that are outside these areas are not coloured.

SHANKILL
This mostly Protestant district is divided from the Falls to the south by wasteland and the city's controversial 'peace' walls. Restoration is planned for the Crumlin Road Courthouse, which suffered a 2009 arson attack. The landmark Crumlin Road Gaol (53-55 Crumlin Road, T 028 9074 1500) hosts events and exhibitions.

QUEEN'S QUARTER
The south is the greenest and most affluent part of town. Highlights include Queen's University campus (see p030 and p074), the Ulster Museum (see p065) situated in the Botanic Gardens, and Lyric Theatre (see p072). Another big draw is the dining and retail strip situated on Lisburn Road.

CATHEDRAL QUARTER
Belfast's flagship district is gathering momentum by the week. Explore its fine arts venues, such as the MAC (see p025) and photography gallery Belfast Exposed (see p028); the slick Merchant Hotel (see p020); and a cluster of intimate drinking dens including The Spaniard (see p062).

TITANIC QUARTER
Of all the city's regeneration projects, this is the most ambitious. The former shipyard is now a 75-hectare leisure, residential and commercial scheme that aims to secure £1bn of investment over the next two decades. And there are nautical attractions (see p031 and p034) aplenty.

FALLS
Largely Catholic, the Falls' Gaeltacht Quarter is now being touted as Belfast's Irish language and culture zone. Visit for the pubs and the exhibitions at Cultúrlann McAdam Ó Fiaich (216 Falls Road, T 028 9096 4180). Divis Tower (see p012) is a reminder of the area's past; its leisure centre (see p092) points to the future.

ORMEAU
This southern suburb is the new Lisburn Road, its redeveloped former bakery now home to businesses such as Boden Park Coffee Company (Unit 10, Ormeau Road, T 077 1608 3085). Stroll to Ormeau Park, which was sold off to the city in 1869 by a debt-ridden Marquess of Donegall.

CITY CENTRE
With its broad avenues, and Victorian and Edwardian architecture, this 19th-century area is a monument to Belfast's industrial past. Dominating the district is City Hall (see p014). East is Custom House Square, the 1865 Albert Memorial Clock (its lean rectified) and a regenerated Laganside.

EAST BELFAST
Belfast's residential east mushroomed during the early 20th century as industry boomed. Mainly Protestant, the area is lined with murals (see p013) revealing the strength of feeling behind unionist and loyalist campaigns. The pioneering Skainos Project (see p066) is building bridges.

LANDMARKS
THE SHAPE OF THE CITY SKYLINE

This city is so forward-facing that the new Belfast only exists fully in the mind of urban planners. To grasp the vision, head up to the viewing platform in Victoria Square (see p068). Look north to Cave Hill (its profile is said to have inspired *Gulliver's Travels*) in order to imagine Giant's Park, a proposed 14-hectare business and green space. Divis Tower (see p012), to the west, flags the Gaeltacht Quarter, and east is Sir Arnold Thornley's neoclassical parliament building, Stormont (Upper Newtownards Road, T 028 9052 1802), the location of the signing of the Good Friday Agreement.

The stainless-steel spire of St Anne's (Donegall Street) marks the Cathedral Quarter. By 2018, Feilden Clegg Bradley Studios' £250m University of Ulster campus will teem with 15,000 students; a £360m mixed-use project, Royal Exchange, is planned for its doorstep. To the north-east stand Harland and Wolff's Samson and Goliath cranes (overleaf), trumpeting the Titanic Quarter (see p031). From your eyrie, you'll also spy Belfast's biggest planning crime – its love affair with cars. Highways riddle the centre and split off the eastern and western suburbs. A forthcoming £100m transit network should encourage these economically depressed areas into the fold. Hidden from view are the narrow 17th-century lanes where it all began. Entrepreneurs congregated in the 'entries' around High Street, propelling the city to industrial greatness.
For full addresses, see Resources.

Samson and Goliath
These canary-yellow cranes are the city's defining landmarks. Curiously omnipresent (they seem to accompany you wherever you are in the centre), the Krupp-Ardelt structures symbolised investment in the local shipbuilding industry during the late 1960s in the face of foreign competition, and a decline in orders. Capable of lifting 840 tonnes, the 96m Goliath (background) was set to work in 1969, and was joined by the 106m Samson (foreground) in 1974. At the time of construction, Harland and Wolff was still one of the world's largest shipbuilders, having turned out aircraft, tankers, trains and, of course, RMS Titanic. Today, the last Olympic-class liners have long since floated down the Lagan, but the cranes are still in use, helping the company service contracts in marine engineering.
Queen's Island, www.harland-wolff.com

011

LANDMARKS

Divis Tower

A notorious Troubles flashpoint, west Belfast's Divis Tower is all that remains of an ambitious social housing project built from 1966 to 1972 to accommodate a swelling population. The lattice of high-rises was demolished in the 1990s, but Frank Robertson's 61m Divis Tower stands defiant. The building's position in-between the unionist Shankill and nationalist Falls areas made it a strategic vantage point for the British Army, which occupied the 18th and 19th floors for three decades from the 1970s to monitor paramilitary activity. Helicopters frequently landed on the roof, but this being Belfast, it was business as usual below, with the lower floors still occupied by tenants. In 2009, the top storeys resumed their function as residences as part of a £1.1m refurb.
Divis Street

Murals

Belfast's murals are potent reminders of the city's sectarianism. From the historical (a 1690 King Billy rearing on his steed) to the disturbing (balaclaved paramilitaries), they mark extant territories and loyalties across town. Now they are attractions in their own right, drawing tourists to points along Newtownards Road (above), and across the Shankill and the Falls. Efforts to replace calls to arms with cultural images have met with varying success. In 2010, an Inverwood Court Ulster Volunteer Force mural was painted over with an image of George Best, only to be daubed again with a UVF slogan. The new breed is gaining ground, though: Aslan roars on Dee Street celebrating local CS Lewis, and a wider political net is cast on Divis Street with riffs on Cuba, Palestine and the Basque Country. *www.belfast-murals.co.uk*

014

City Hall

This baroque behemoth, reopened in 2009 after an £11m refit by architects Consarc, signposts the heart of Belfast. Alfred Brumwell Thomas' 1906 building crowned an elegant new city, sealing its transformation from industrial arriviste to confident metropolis. The Portland stone and 53m dome are illuminated for civic celebrations. Tours are available.
Donegall Square, T 028 9027 0456

HOTELS

WHERE TO STAY AND WHICH ROOMS TO BOOK

Despite the recent explosion in civic spectacles and events, the international traveller has to work hard to find a roost in this town. After the wilderness of the Troubles, the accommodation scene started to look up from 2004, when Malmaison (opposite) and Ten Square (see p023) blazed trails with Belfast's first boutique boltholes. The Merchant Hotel (see p020) upped the ante two years later, introducing some five-star sophistication and opulence to the newly minted Cathedral Quarter. Pushing the city's room tally beyond the 6,000 mark were biscuit-toned arrivals from the likes of Hilton and Ibis, with the 2004 Radisson Blu (The Gasworks, 3 Cromac Place, Ormeau Road, T 028 9043 4065) proving the most imaginative of the bunch. For the city to become a true contender, though, there will have to be more properties in a similar vein to the new £12m four-star hotel due to open in the former Scottish Mutual Building on Donegall Square South in 2016, courtesy of the Hill family of Ballymena's Galgorm Resort fame.

If all the decent rooms in the city centre are booked, consider heading a little further out to the four-star Park Avenue (158 Holywood Road, T 028 9065 6520), close to City Airport, Il Pirata (see p055) and CS Lewis' local church, St Mark's. Meanwhile, a 20-minute cab ride east, there's the Culloden (Bangor Road, Holywood, T 028 9042 1066), a bishop's palace turned five-star retreat.

For full addresses and room rates, see Resources.

Malmaison
When the musicians hit town for gigs like Belsonic, the rooms here are the first to be snapped up. Originally a 19th-century seed warehouse, and formerly the McCausland Hotel, the property was transformed by Malmaison. The 64 guest rooms, initially designed by Jestico + Whiles and recently refurbished by Katrine Bradley, are done out in the chain's flamboyant gothic style, all gilt frames, black beams and darkwood furniture. Twisting the rock 'n' roll dial further are the two suites with gas fires, Samson (above) and Goliath; the former also has a snooker table. Peter Lavery's photos add a note of restraint with images of industrial Belfast. Skip the marine-themed brasserie and head to the Malbar for one of Malmaison's signature cocktails. *34-38 Victoria Street, T 0844 693 0650, www.malmaison.com*

The Fitzwilliam Hotel
Housing Belfast's most expensive room (the penthouse on the eighth floor will set you back a cool £1,500 a night), Jim and June Burgess' 2009 hotel is the most ebullient member of the city's hospitality scene, attracting celebrities and business types with deep pockets. Interior designers Project Orange selected a palette of black and mustard, orange and red for the 133 guest rooms, which are all decorated with Bridget Riley-esque pieces by Spires Art. Next to the Levanto marble reception is a living room-style lobby (left) with nice touches: Project Orange's high-backed winged chairs sit in front of a flickering fire and shelves are lined with good tomes. For the best views across town, reserve one of the corner Deluxe Rooms.
Great Victoria Street, T 028 9044 2080, www.fitzwilliamhotelbelfast.com

The Merchant Hotel
Wrought out of James Hamilton's 1860 Ulster Bank headquarters by architects Consarc, Bill Wolsey's hotel launched with 21 rooms and five suites. Ann-Marie O'Neill injected lavish Victoriana throughout, using chocolate hues, gilt mirrors, velvet headboards and marble bathrooms (installed with Lefroy Brooks thermostatic showers powerful enough to hose down an elephant). In 2010, a £16.5m 38-room extension, with art deco-style interiors, swept in roll-top baths and illuminated mirrors. If the suites are booked, opt for a Deluxe Room (above), or 529, which has a walk-in wardrobe. In the Great Room's restaurant (opposite), you'll see Ireland's biggest chandelier, designed by Marcus Notley. There is also a classy cocktail lounge, a nightclub and a jazz bar (see p052), all delivering impeccable service.
16 Skipper Street, T 028 9023 4888, www.themerchanthotel.com

021

HOTELS

Europa

Battered but not beaten, this 1971 four-star is the embodiment of Belfast's highs and lows. The most bombed hotel in western Europe (putting up journalists attracted 33 blasts during the Troubles) has for four decades been *the* venue for family and corporate gatherings. Designed by Sydney Kaye, Eric Firkin & Partners, and built for a then mind-boggling sum of £2m, the Europa is now prospering under general manager James McGinn, thanks to its cheery service. We forgive its exterior mishmash of 12-storey tower block and appliqué columns, added as part of Robinson Patterson Partnership's 1990s renovation, and applaud Brian Gorman's interior refurb. Follow Hillary Clinton's lead and reserve the Titanic Suite (above). *Great Victoria Street, T 028 9027 1066, www.hastingshotels.com/europa-belfast*

Ten Square

Occupying a coveted location opposite City Hall (see p014), this 1863 linenmaster's warehouse was converted into a hotel in 2004 by United Design, who provided an on-trend oriental-style interior: Belfast could finally cater for the design-savvy metrophile. Today, we have a different beast. Manager Kevin Smyth kept the business alive during the recession with cut-price deals, and the two-for-one party atmosphere still lingers with hen packages, free buffets, and bargain beer during rugby and football screenings. The 22 rooms, now categorised as 'cosy', 'wonderful' and 'fabulous', have lost some of their original design focus. That said, a 2014 renovation, overseen by Smyth, promises a significant upgrade. Book the Linenhall Suite (above).
*10 Donegall Square South,
T 028 9024 1001, www.tensquare.co.uk*

24 HOURS
SEE THE BEST OF THE CITY IN JUST ONE DAY

It's not lost on locals that two of Belfast's most enticing attractions are born of strife and tragedy. The town that built RMS Titanic, regarded for so long as a mark of shame, now celebrates the White Star Line icon with an impressive exhibition (see p034). Open-top buses and cabs crisscross the suburbs, providing insights into the city's sectarian history with voyeuristic peeks at deprived estates, murals (see p013) and 'peace' walls. Both experiences paint a vital broader canvas: Belfast as a post-industrial city with the misfortune of being situated on an ethno-political faultline.

Our day starts with a caffeine-enhanced orientation session at the MAC (opposite), the arts centre beaten to the 2013 Stirling Prize by the Giant's Causeway Visitor Centre (see p098). Head round the corner to Commercial Court to see the province's most famous sons and daughters in a courtyard painted by Danny Devenney and Marty Lyons, and depicting Seamus Heaney, Mary Peters and Van Morrison among others. Next, visit two cutting-edge galleries (see p026 and p028), before hopping in a cab for a short ride south to lunch at Michael Deane's breezy restaurant (see p029). Then it's over the Lagan to explore the Titanic legacy (see p031). The Crown Liquor Saloon (see p036), which boasts an exotic interior fashioned by Italian craftsmen, is our stop-off for a tipple before dinner at contemporary restaurant OX (see p038).

For full addresses, see Resources.

10.00 MAC
This 2012 complex is the brightest symbol of the 'new Belfast', and its excellent café is the best place to begin your day. The brief was to provide a culture-hungry city with a democratic, central space for the contemporary arts. Architects Hackett Hall McKnight slid a sinewy amalgam of brick, concrete and Antrim basalt on to an old car park, topping it with a lantern tower. Beyond the atrium (above), adorned with Mark Garry's *The Permanent Present* installation, there are six floors housing studios, two theatres and three galleries, showing work by international artists such as Peter Doig and locals like photographer Mary McIntyre. The furniture is also well curated; you'll spy Bedont's 'Drive' chairs and Maurizio Galante's 'Cactus' stools.
10 Exchange Street West, T 028 9023 5053, www.themaclive.com

11.00 **Catalyst Arts Gallery**

Tucked down a desolate side street, this gallery is the wellspring of Belfast's contemporary art scene. Founded in 1993 and based at this former skate park since 2010, its founding director was the Turner Prize winner Susan Philipsz; some of its curators have gone on to launch other art venues such as Golden Thread (T 028 9033 0920) and Satis House (T 07921 072 309), and annual festival HouseHold. At Catalyst, 10 volunteer directors work at breakneck pace, organising up to 20 shows a year in the main gallery ('con-glom-er-ate', above) and in a project space for experimental work. There are exchanges with galleries across Ireland, the UK, Finland and France, and a local outreach programme. Open Tuesday to Saturday, 11am to 5pm.
Ground floor, 5 College Court,
T 028 9031 3303, www.catalystarts.org.uk

12.00 Belfast Exposed
Launched in 1983, this photography gallery put cameras in the hands of locals, encouraging them to document ordinary life during the Troubles. The intention was to counterbalance the sensationalist coverage generated by journalists who dipped in and out for a few hours. Three decades on, the archive holds 500,000 images. The aim remains the same: to use photography to engage citizens through training and community projects. Now occupying a former shirt factory near The Merchant Hotel (see p020), the gallery comprises a bookshop and a space for shows by established photographers such as Taryn Simon, the late Allan Sekula and Mark Curran ('The Market', above). Open Tuesday to Saturday, 11am to 4pm.
The Exchange Place, 23 Donegall Street, T 028 9023 0965, www.belfastexposed.org

13.00 Deanes at Queens
Formerly a common room for Queen's University staff, this 2008 restaurant is our choice of Michael Deane's various Belfast venues. Interior designers Triplicate were responsible for the airy space, which pulls in the well-heeled Malone Road set. The walls are decorated with portraits of Deane, his sommelier and his venison supplier, all by artist and illustrator Oliver Jeffers. Manager Saul McConnell runs a tight ship, powered by head chef Chris Fearon, who trained under Brian McCann of Shu (see p056). Regarding his culinary style, Fearon says: 'I'm a country lad, so it's an honest approach – what I would like to eat at home.' Expect pragmatic yet graceful dishes on the menu, such as salt and chilli squid, and crisp pork belly. *1 College Gardens, T 028 9038 2111, www.michaeldeane.co.uk*

14.30 Queen's University

It took some eight decades for Queen's campus to free itself from the grip of Charles Lanyon's neo-Gothic aesthetic, his 1849 centrepiece setting the trend for all manner of Victorian frippery. Rapid postwar expansion opened the door to a host of modernist and contemporary newcomers. Take in Thomas Lodge's David Keir Building (39-123 Stranmillis Road), a 1959 neo-Georgian colossus, and 2002 additions such as Todd Architects' McClay Research Centre (Jubilee Road) and Hall Black Douglas' Sonic Arts Research Centre (4 Cloreen Park). Our pick is Cruickshank & Seward's Ashby Institute (above; 125 Stranmillis Road), a 1965 structure whose white-limestone render and diamond faceting trump its red-brick neighbours with an International Style flourish.
www.qub.ac.uk

15.30 Titanic's Dock & Pump-House

This 1904 pump-house (above) and dry dock (overleaf) bring to life the industrial heft and mind-boggling scale of the Titanic. At nearly 274m long, the ship floated into this berth in February 1912; the dock was then drained to allow workers to paint her hull and fit three huge bronze propellers. Today, you can wander among the keel blocks that propped up the liner's 46,000-plus tonnes, and marvel at the 1,000-tonne caisson gate used to seal the dock. Enter the pump-house to see the technology that made it all happen: an 80-tonne hydraulic accumulator provided the power to open the gate, and a trio of Gwynnes Pumps could suck the dock dry of its 23 million gallons in an hour and 40 minutes. Films are occasionally screened here.
Queen's Road, Queen's Island, T 028 9073 7813, www.titanicsdock.com

Titanic's Dry Dock

033

24 HOURS

16.00 Titanic Belfast

The city was relatively late to the Titanic goldrush, when exhibitions popped up worldwide following James Cameron's 1997 blockbuster. But Belfast has made up for it with this £97m complex, opened in 2012 where 15,000 Harland and Wolff workers built the opulent liner. Ghoulish money-spinners aside (Titanic Porthole cookie anyone?), the display is a moving evocation of the ambition, hubris and technical skill surrounding both the ship's creation and demise. Inside the CivicArts & Todd-designed building, whose 'towers' echo Titanic's prow, are six floors taking you from Belfast's shipyard boom to the haunting SOS messages that floated through the Atlantic fog on the night of 14 April 1912. *1 Olympic Way, Queen's Road, T 028 9076 6386, www.titanicbelfast.com*

19.00 The Crown Liquor Saloon

Its tourist throng diluted by loyal Belfast imbibers, the Crown has an extraordinary interior. Now managed by Nicholson's Will Elliott and owned by the National Trust, the pub started life as the ordinary Railway Tavern in 1826. In 1884, the landlord's son, Patrick Flanigan, went on the 19th-century equivalent of a backpacking trip, returning with a head full of foreign designs. Italian craftsmen were set to work creating papier moulded snakeskin pillars, doorposts alive with phoenixes and lions, and stained glass dripping with bunches of grapes. Arrive early to bag one of the nine snugs (the 10th was dismantled to make way for a ladies' loo) and order a Guinness. If you want to stay for a bite to eat, Jimmy Jenkins dishes up good modern pub food. *46 Great Victoria Street, T 028 9024 3187, www.nicholsonspubs.co.uk*

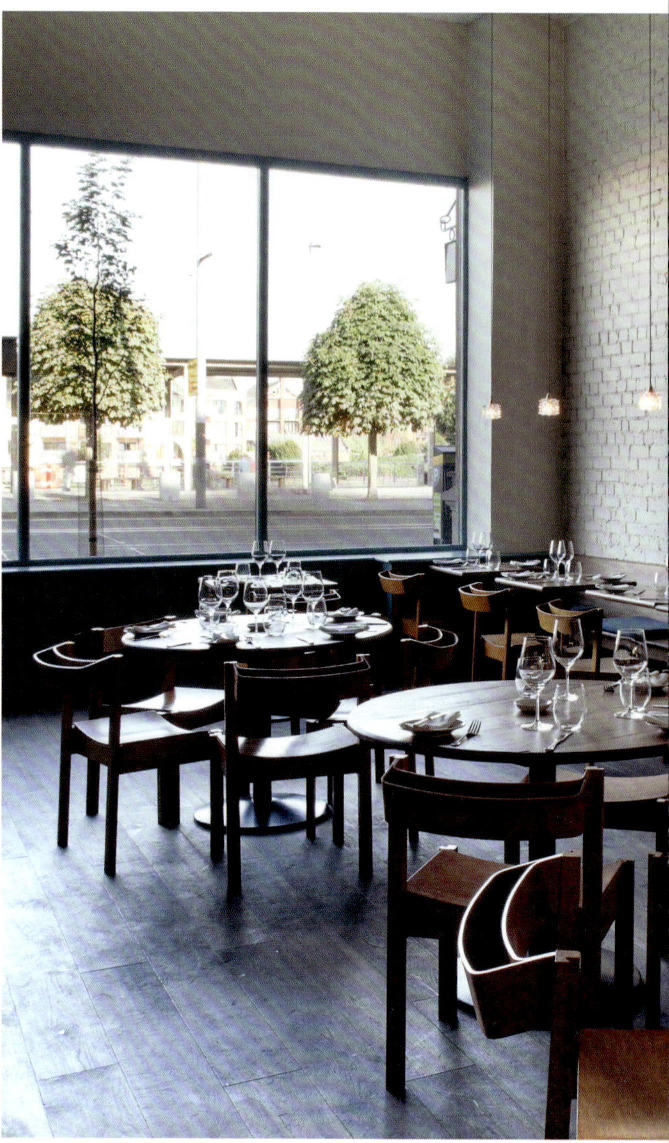

20.00 OX

Opening in a former Laganside tile shop in 2013, this pared-back two-floor restaurant marked a turning point in Belfast's dining scene. OX's Brittany-born manager, Alain Kerloc'h, and Stephen Toman, former head chef at James Street South (see p048), devised an upmarket foraged menu that celebrates the clean flavours of neglected ingredients such as homemade milk curd, verbena and pollan, a freshwater fish that swims in Lough Neagh. Oscar&Oscar, who also designed Il Pirata (see p055), created a reclaimed, semi-industrial aesthetic using church chairs, clapboard and painted brickwork; we admire the reuse of tiles found in the original shop as breadboards. Our dinner order included salty clams with artichokes, amaranth and sauvignon blanc foam, followed by Bushmills jelly with apple and lavender.
1 Oxford Street, T 028 9031 4121, www.oxbelfast.com

URBAN LIFE
CAFÉS, RESTAURANTS, BARS AND NIGHTCLUBS

Belfast's bars and restaurants play to the city's greatest strengths: its warmth and unpretentiousness. The dearth of Michelin stars points to a diner happier with a simple bowl of mussels rather than high-falutin' foams and fusions – Michael Deane's Howard Street flagship (see p054) lost Northern Ireland's sole bauble in 2010. Recession woes diminished, the culinary scene is flourishing. For every historic pub such as Bittles Bar (70 Upper Church Lane), there are sophisticated openings like OX (see p038).

This being Belfast, a select coterie is making it happen. Emma Bricknell of Made in Belfast (opposite) has also hatched Le Coop (38 Hill Street, T 028 9545 8120); Niall McKenna of James Street South (see p048) opened Hadskis (33 Donegall Street/Commercial Court, T 028 9032 5444); and Love & Death (see p046) gained sibling Aether & Echo (11 Lower Garfield Street, T 028 9023 9163). No one can rival Bill Wolsey, though. His 2014 Dirty Onion will capitalise on the student influx from the new University of Ulster campus. Despite all this industry, there is a distinct lack of crowds, a hangover from the centre's garrisoned days. The hordes flock to The John Hewitt (51 Donegall Street, T 028 9023 3768) and the Duke of York (7-11 Commercial Court, T 028 9024 1062). End your evening with live music and a pint of Guinness at the 18th-century Kelly's Cellars (30-32 Bank Street, T 028 9024 6058).

For full addresses, see Resources.

Made in Belfast

Globetrotter Emma Bricknell landed in the city centre in 2008, launching her first Made in Belfast (T 028 9024 6712) close to City Hall (see p014). This 2011 follow-up brings a car crash of mismatched furniture and 1950s quiffs to the Cathedral Quarter. The local/eco mantra is hammered home at every turn (the menu has outdoor-bred bacon and sustainable seafood chowder), and thankfully the flavours live up to the pitch. Try the Dundrum potted crab on wheaten bread. The only way to survive the interior of fake leopard-skin sofa, bowler-hat pendant and industrial ceiling plastered with magazine cuttings is to order an Irish Martini, made with Jameson whisky and clove-infused dry vermouth. A spirited, under-40 crowd dominates. *23 Talbot Street, T 028 9024 4107, www.madeinbelfastni.com*

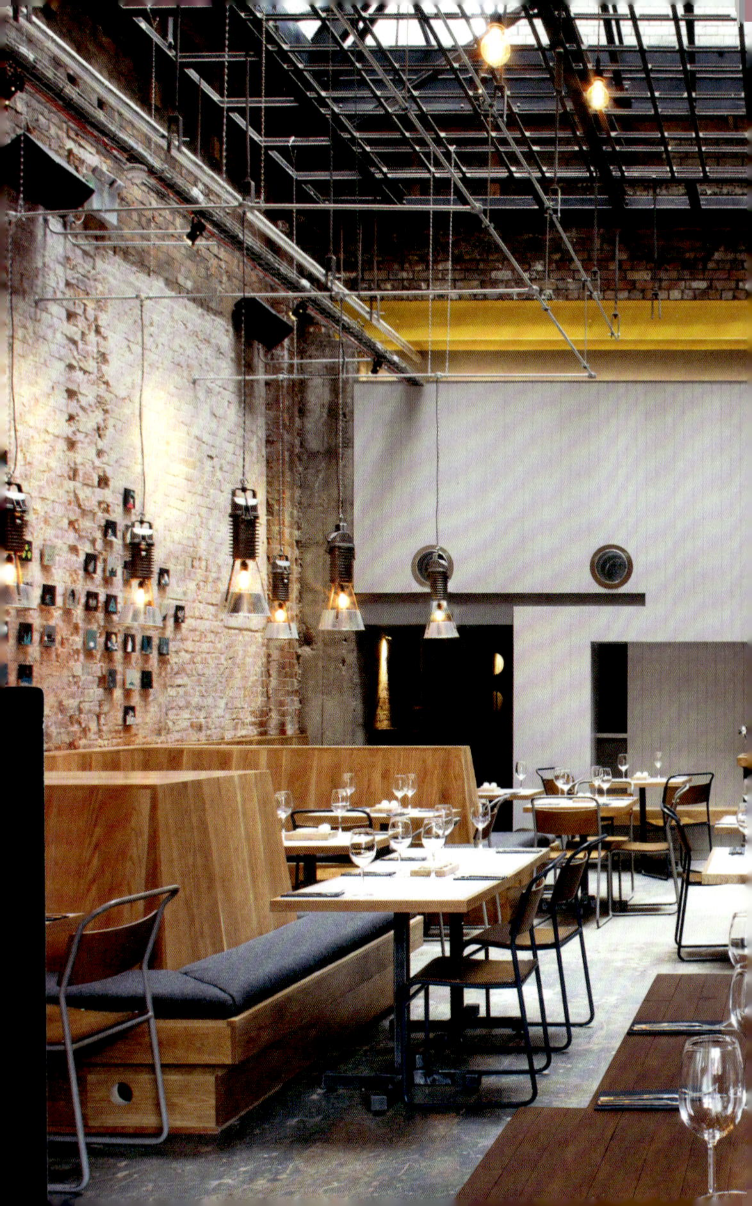

The National Grande Café
Bill Wolsey opened this venue in 2013, in a former National Bank building. Consarc's John Busteed designed the cavernous interior, its original Victorian innards exposed in the form of yellow girders and brickwork. Supplying the baked goods is Wolsey's Pâtisserie Mimi, located next door. A high-end club is due to launch upstairs in 2014.
62-68 High Street, T 028 9031 1130

URBAN LIFE

Cafe Mauds
Founded in 1982, Mauds is the byword for top-quality ice cream across Northern Ireland, bagging 129 awards and churning out moreish honeycomb, chocolate and classic vanilla creations by the tonne. John Pell, who owns another Mauds (T 028 9332 9988) down the road in Newcastle, County Down, and has exclusive rights to distribute this frozen gold throughout the Republic of Ireland, set up this buzzy café in 2011, after a five-year hunt for the right address. The angular interior, designed by Exhibit, is softened by chalkboards, rustic stone walls and black-and-white photos of contented diners. Also serving a good selection of muffins, bagels, crepes and sundaes, it's a hub of ladies-who-lunch and kids, and a popular (alcohol-free) evening rendezvous.
555 Lisburn Road, T 028 9543 8486, www.mauds.co.uk

Mourne Seafood Bar

Until a decade ago, Belfast was sniffy about shellfish. Enter Bob McCoubrey's 2006 restaurant and now the city's diners can't get enough of rope-grown mussels from Strangford Lough, lobsters from Kilkeel and Pacific oysters from Donegal. Situated adjacent to Kelly's Cellars (see p040), this 120-seat restaurant is famous for its egalitarian following, barristers, office workers and visitors all enjoying the scallop linguine or crab-stuffed peppers. Upstairs, there's a cookery school and an oyster bar, where McCoubrey's brick interior is decorated with paintings by local artist James G Miles. To drink, try a glass of Mourne Oyster stout, which was formulated by McCoubrey, head chef Andy Rae and Whitewater Brewery.
34-36 Bank Street, T 028 9024 8544, www.mourneseafood.com

Love & Death
Inspired by a quote from chef Ferran Adrià – 'Nothing is serious apart from love. Love and death' – this is the thinking man's decadent retreat. Owned by Brian McGeown and Anthony Farrell, it has two madcap floors sprayed with graffiti by local KVLR, festooned with action figures suspended from the ceiling and furnished with giant electrical-cable reels that function as tables. Despite the ramshackle feel, you will come across old ladies and the odd high-court judge tucking into lunches of meat liquor-soaked sarnies and chilli hotdogs in the first-floor bar. On Thursday, Friday and Saturday nights, the top floor hosts DJ sets, while some of the best-looking barmen in town serve up basil-tinged gin, nitrous oxide-infused Zombies and the whisky-based sour, Belfast Black and Blue.
10a Anne Street, T 028 9024 7222, www.loveanddeathinc.com

047

URBAN LIFE

James Street South

Niall McKenna has worked for the likes of Marco Pierre White and cooked for Al Pacino and Prince Charles. So no wonder his restaurant, hewn out of a linen store by Aidan McGrath, is quietly assured. The pared-down seasonal menu follows suit. After dinner, go next door to his Bar + Grill (T 028 9560 0700); try barman John McCann's Cardamom and Honey Smash.
21 James Street South, T 028 9043 4310

URBAN LIFE

The Potted Hen

Despite the mixed reaction to the new £100m St Anne's Square (dismissed by some as neoclassical pastiche), the public space is meeting its brief as a social and cultural hub. An essential ingredient is Dermot and Catherine Regan's bistro, founded in 2010 and the first restaurant on the block. Head chef James Neill cooks modern Irish fare; try a Delmonico steak from Mark Hix-favourite Peter Hannan, who dry-ages his meat in a chamber made of salt bricks from the Himalayas. The interior, by McCue of Carrickfergus, is minimal, its centrepiece a brazen air-conditioning duct. Skip the ground-floor area and head upstairs for good views of the square and softer banquette seating that absorbs the cacophony.
Edward Street, T 028 9023 4554, www.thepottedhen.co.uk

Robinson & Cleaver

This location is a retail legend. Edward Robinson and John Cleaver opened their department store in 1888, commissioning Young & MacKenzie to convert a linen warehouse in Belfast's grand new centre. The city's smartest shop closed in 1984, its iconic marble staircase later auctioned off. Thanks to Andy Watt, formerly of Yellow Door (T 028 9038 1961), older shoppers can relive memories of hunting for skunk stoles and fine Irish linen in a slither of the building, converted in 2013 by architects McGonigle McGrath. Downstairs is a deli (T 028 9031 2538) and upstairs there's a bar and an airy restaurant. The prize spot is the terrace (above), which overlooks City Hall (see p014), and has heaters and blankets to counter those brisk easterlies. *Donegall Square North, T 028 9031 2666, www.robinsonandcleaver.com*

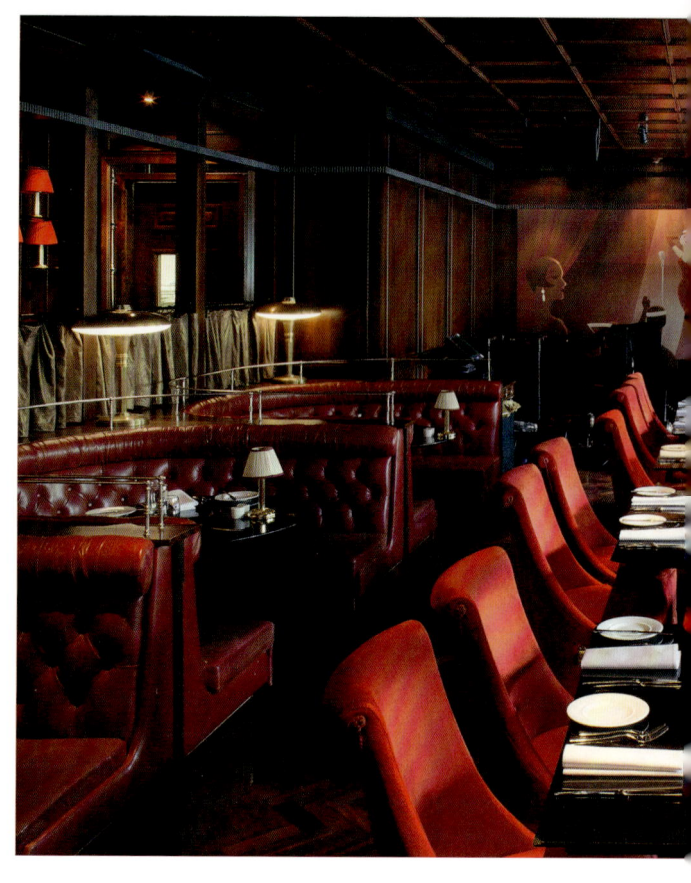

Berts

In the wrong hands, this jazz bar in The Merchant Hotel (see p020) could miss the mark. But with Anne Marie O'Neill at the interiors helm and Kyron Bourke in charge of bands and solo artists, it's another coup for Bill Wolsey. The vibe is 1930s – boater- and bow-tie-sporting waiters make busy at a horseshoe chrome bar, and the retro bistro-style menu offers dishes such as Waldorf salad and coquilles St Jacques.

Among the best cocktails are the Corpse Reviver No2, featuring Hennessy VS and chartreuse, and the Penicillin, sluiced with Johnnie Walker Red Label and Tobermory Isle of Mull malts. As with all good venues across the city, the crowd is mixed, older couples happy to share the red-leather banquettes with nattily dressed hipsters.
*16 Skipper Street, T 028 9026 2713,
www.themerchanthotel.com*

053

URBAN LIFE

Deanes

From washing pots at Claridge's to a 13-year run of Michelin stars, Michael Deane is Belfast's highest-profile chef. The jewel of his restaurant empire is the formal Deanes, where head chef Simon Toye teases local fare into artful plates of seared scallops, Lissara duck breast, and tomato broth with poached lobster and chervil. Occupying the interior, which was spruced up in 2013 by Deane and his wife, Kate Smith, is a deal-clinching business crowd, leavened by younger TV and ad agency types. For a lighter atmosphere, visit Deanes Deli Vin Cafe (T 028 9024 8830), which serves fairly priced carafes and small plates, such as whitebait with green chilli aioli, by head chef Craig McCoy. There's live music on Friday and Saturday evenings.
36-40 Howard Street, T 028 9033 1134, www.michaeldeane.co.uk

Coppi

On paper it was madness: turn a drab KFC on a moribund East Belfast strip into a trendy restaurant; shun both phone line and sign, and rely solely on social media for publicity. Against the odds, enthusiastic cyclists Tony O'Neill and Sam Spain rode to victory with their 2011 venue Il Pirata (T 028 9067 3421). The restaurant, named after Italian cycling legend Marco Pantani, and with interiors by Oscar & Oscar (open kitchen, white tiles, and industrial-style lighting), introduced a new aesthetic to the city. The duo struck out again in 2012 with Coppi (above), which has furniture from Terry (see p086). Venetian-style *cicchetti* of duck ragu and fritto misto have been flying out of both kitchens ever since, along with top-class cocktails.
St Anne's Square, T 028 9031 1959, www.coppi.co.uk

Shu

Alan Reid's Lisburn Road institution has been concocting high-end cuisine since 2000. Over three floors, the Japanese-influenced interior by Paul Horscroft serves as a counterweight to Brian McCann's colourful European cooking. The main restaurant (pictured) attracts an affluent, older clientele, whereas the downstairs area draws a younger crowd.
253 Lisburn Road, T 028 9038 1655

URBAN LIFE

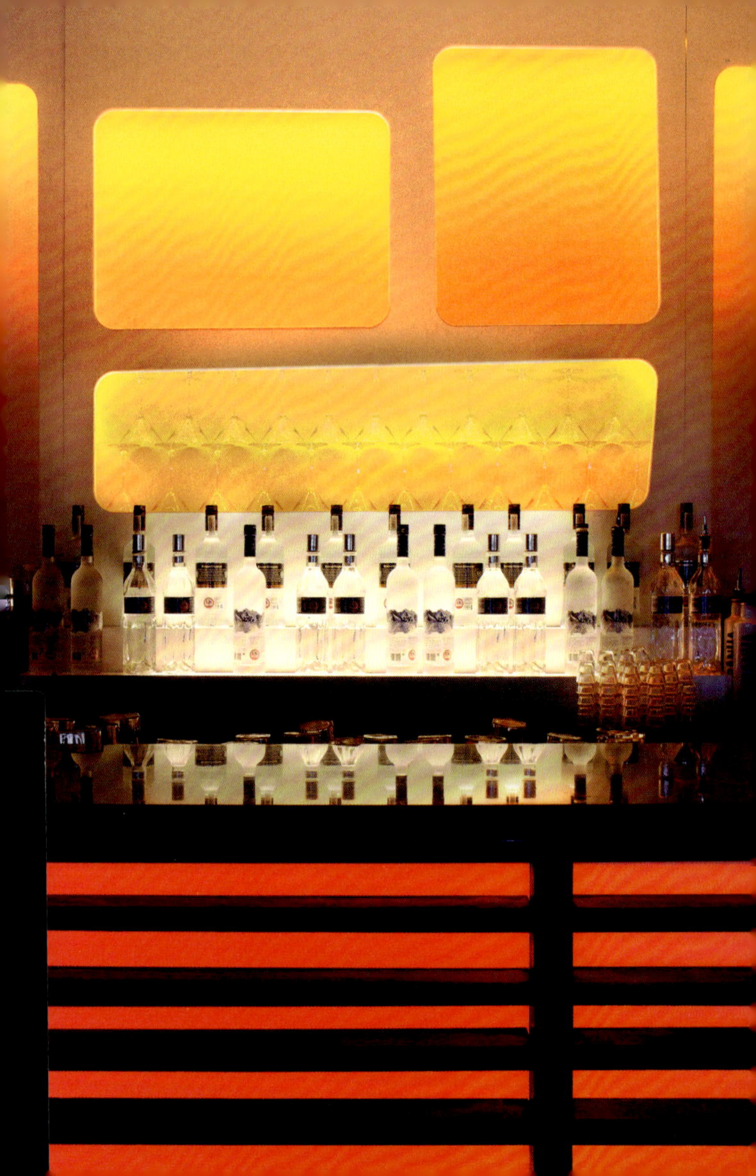

El Divino

Bringing the Ibiza franchise to Belfast, this Laganside club was founded by Paul Langsford in 2011. A million-pound investment resulted in a three-storey 'superclub'. There's a ground-level lounge (opposite), an intimate Little Disco, and Green Room (above) for performers and their coterie on the first floor, and a top-floor main club; all the interiors are by architects Donnelly O Neill. The club area has a 109cm Emulator, a Starship Enterprise-style MIDI controller that was the first to touch down in Ireland. Go to check out aerial dance routines and star DJ sets by the likes of Roger Sanchez and Mark Knight, and locals Steve Turnbull, Jon Boi and Hix. For £1,000, you can party like a celeb with a private bar and security.
*Mays Meadow, T 028 9032 2000,
www.eldivino-belfast.com*

Muriel's Café Bar

Its interiors modelled on a Victorian gin palace, this is the Cathedral Quarter's first-date hotspot. Owner Janine Kane has created a ground-floor resembling a frou-frou milliner's shop and an upstairs space (above) evoking the ambience of a private box in a Victorian music hall, with crushed-velvet stools, peacock feathers and candelabra. The selection of gins takes star billing, thanks to the hard-to-find labels on offer, such as French G'Vine, Brockmans and Monkey 47 with its multifarious botanicals. To soak up all the libations, there are good cheese and meat platters. Of all the £7.50 cocktails on the drinks list, order the delicious Milliner's Mix. Its precise ingredients are a closely guarded secret and it's usually served in a jam jar.
12-14 Church Lane, T 028 9033 2445

Home Restaurant

Launched in 2011 as a pop-up by Bob McCoubrey and Andy Rae of Mourne Seafood Bar (see p045), together with Steven Haller, this restaurant is now permanent. In the early days, you could dine and walk off with your purchased plate or chair, but today's takeaways are limited to artworks by the likes of Clare Taggart and Fiona McAlpine. The thrifty vibe endures, however. McCoubrey teamed up with ReFound (see p080) to create an interior comprising mismatched lamps and reclaimed chairs. The healthy menu, which makes for a great lunch, is courtesy of head chef Ben Arnold, who spent seven years in London, working in the kitchens of the House of Commons, La Trompette and Le Gavroche.
22 Wellington Place, T 028 9023 4946, www.homepopup.com

INSIDER'S GUIDE
LYNDSEY MCDOUGALL, ARTIST

Artist and part-time lecturer at the University of Ulster, Lyndsey McDougall lives on leafy Ormeau Road on the south side of the city. Seeking fresh ideas, she frequently crosses Botanic Gardens (College Park, Botanic Avenue, T 028 9031 4762) to sketch items in the Ulster Museum (see p065) within the grounds.

McDougall often starts her day with some home-baked goods and an espresso from Bread and Banjo Bakery (353 Ormeau Road, T 07720 961 310). Come lunchtime, she'll head into the centre for a bite at Grapevine (5 Pottingers Entry, T 028 9023 8182): 'leek and potato soup in winter, and a brie and cranberry toastie in summer'. The early afternoon is given over to buying cheese and seafood at Sawers (Fountain Centre, College Street, T 028 9032 2021), followed by a yoga session at Flow Studio (52a Hill Street, T 028 9023 1981). At 6pm sharp, a feisty bloody mary calls at The Spaniard (3 Skipper Street, T 028 9023 2448), settled by a drop of peaty Connemara whisky at folk hotspot the Sunflower (65 Union Street, T 028 9023 2474). Then a quick sharpener ('usually Hilden Brewery's Belfast Blonde') at The Hudson Bar (10-14 Gresham Street, T 028 9023 2322) whets the artist's appetite for a bargain half-lobster at Mourne Seafood Bar (see p045). Her evening draws to a close at the Menagerie (130 University Street, T 028 9023 5678), where she joins 'an arty crowd' enjoying the live music.
For full addresses, see Resources.

URBAN LIFE

ARCHITOUR

A GUIDE TO BELFAST'S ICONIC BUILDINGS

The Troubles stopped a healthy run of modernist architecture in its tracks. The 1972 Ulster Museum extension (opposite) was the last hurrah, before the city became more occupied with patching up bomb-blasted landmarks than constructing them. After a 30-year hiatus, Belfast is playing catch-up. Ambitious new buildings are being wrought out of the red-brick vernacular, the city finally recognising the power of good design to transform communities as well as skylines. The most striking examples of this sea change are the MAC (see p025) and the Skainos Project (see p066), a barrier-bridging community and housing scheme in East Belfast.

Belfast's backbone is Victorian (Charles Lanyon's Gothic Revival hand abounds) and the city is slowly rehabilitating its 19th-century legacy. Part of the old Robinson & Cleaver department store has reopened as a café (see p051), while less stylish interventions have taken place around Donegall Square. It's a shame, though, that so much of Belfast's architectural heritage still sits on the to-do list. Harland and Wolff's majestic drawing offices are currently closed to the public, their innards home to pigeons. A benefactor is needed to stop the Victorian baths at the Templemore Centre (Templemore Avenue, T 028 9045 7540) from disappearing down the plughole, and trees are sprouting out of the glorious former Belfast Banking Company Building (Donegall Street/Waring Street).

For full addresses, see Resources.

Ulster Museum
Hamilton Associates' ambitious £15m revamp has elevated this 1929 museum to greatness. It was already a hybrid; James Cumming Wynnes originally designed a classical building, before Francis Pym bolted on a brutalist extension in 1972. The latest 2009 scheme raised the roof 70m and expanded the exhibition space by 1,225 sq m. The results are dramatic. Stepping on to the glass-sided walkway on the top floor to survey the 23m-high atrium makes you dizzy; dusty cases and academic nomenclature are out, art and nature 'discovery zones' are in. The strong local thread includes exhibitions on Home Rule and landscapes by Belfast painter John Lavery. The impressive café is run by Yellow Door (see p051).
Botanic Gardens, T 028 9044 0000, www.nmni.com/um

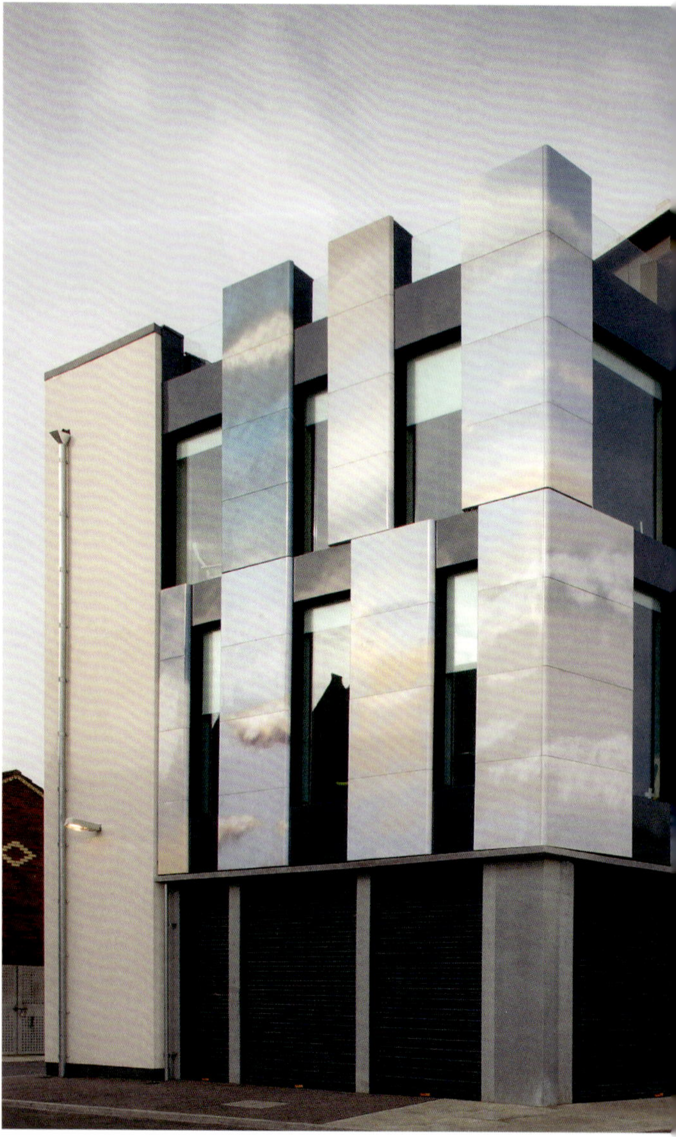

Skainos Project

Donnelly O Neill's £20.6m 'urban village' is an exemplar cross-community project. The centrepiece of the 2012 scheme is a main building of brick and exposed concrete: a cool, calm space for local support groups. Standout eco features include greened facades, solar panels and bird boxes. Artist Jonny McEwen painted the enamel panels (pictured).
239 Newtownards Road, T 028 9073 8989

ARCHITOUR

Victoria Square

Costing £165m, BDP's huge 2008 shopping complex-cum-tourist attraction represents the high-water mark of Belfast's retail scene. Numerous big brands stayed away during the Troubles, and Victoria Square signalled the city was open for business. Renaissance hyperbole aside, the centre is a genuine landmark, a sweeping wood-and-brick structure of open and closed 'streets', leading to a viewing platform encased by a glass dome. Take a moment to adjust to the rostrum's subtle movement (all within acceptable engineering limits, of course). Knitting the site together is a river-style ribbon, three blue tiles wide, trickling along at ground level. Nearly 63,000 sq m of space houses middle- and upmarket chains, a cinema and eateries.
1 Victoria Square, T 028 9032 2277, www.victoriasquare.com

Waterfront Hall

This 1997 arts and conference rotunda was the city's first major civic project since the 1930s. Robinson McIlwaine's building is the kingpin of an ambitious Laganside regeneration scheme designed to reclaim a derelict part of the river snaking around the centre. Nearly half the facade is glass, blurring the boundaries between venue, street and water. Inside, there's a 380-seat studio, a restaurant, bars and exhibition space. The centrepiece is the 2,223-seat auditorium, created by the architects Carr & Angier and Sandy Brown Associates, and rated by some as the most versatile concert hall in Europe. Hosting music, theatre, ballet and opera performances, the venue is now famous thanks to its backdrop role in BBC TV drama *The Fall*.
2 Lanyon Place, T 028 9033 4400,
www.waterfront.co.uk

Grand Opera House

Paramilitaries and property developers have both tried to wreck this venue, but Frank Matcham's superb 1895 landmark has survived the onslaught, its oriental, baroque and Flemish exterior heralding the glories within. It was earmarked for development in the early 1970s, but the Ulster Architectural Society stepped in to help make the opera house Northern Ireland's first listed building. In the early 1990s, car bombs pummelled the dressing rooms, prompting the installation of blast walls. The main auditorium has curvaceous balconies and Indian-style trompe l'oeil ceiling panels by artist Cherith McKinstry, created as part of Robert McKinstry & Melvyn Brown's 1980 restoration. In 2006, Arts Team's controversial boxy extension, known as Act II, bolted on a new foyer, dressing rooms, a bar and a café.
Great Victoria Street, T 028 9024 1919, www.goh.co.uk

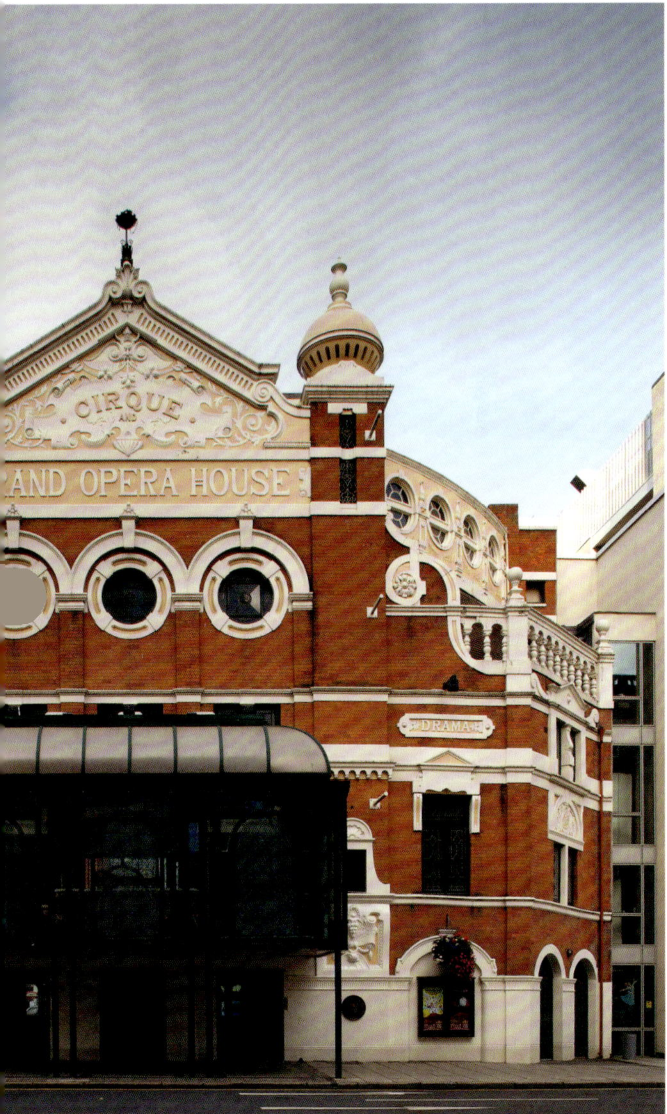
CIRQUE
AND
AND OPERA HOUSE
DRAMA

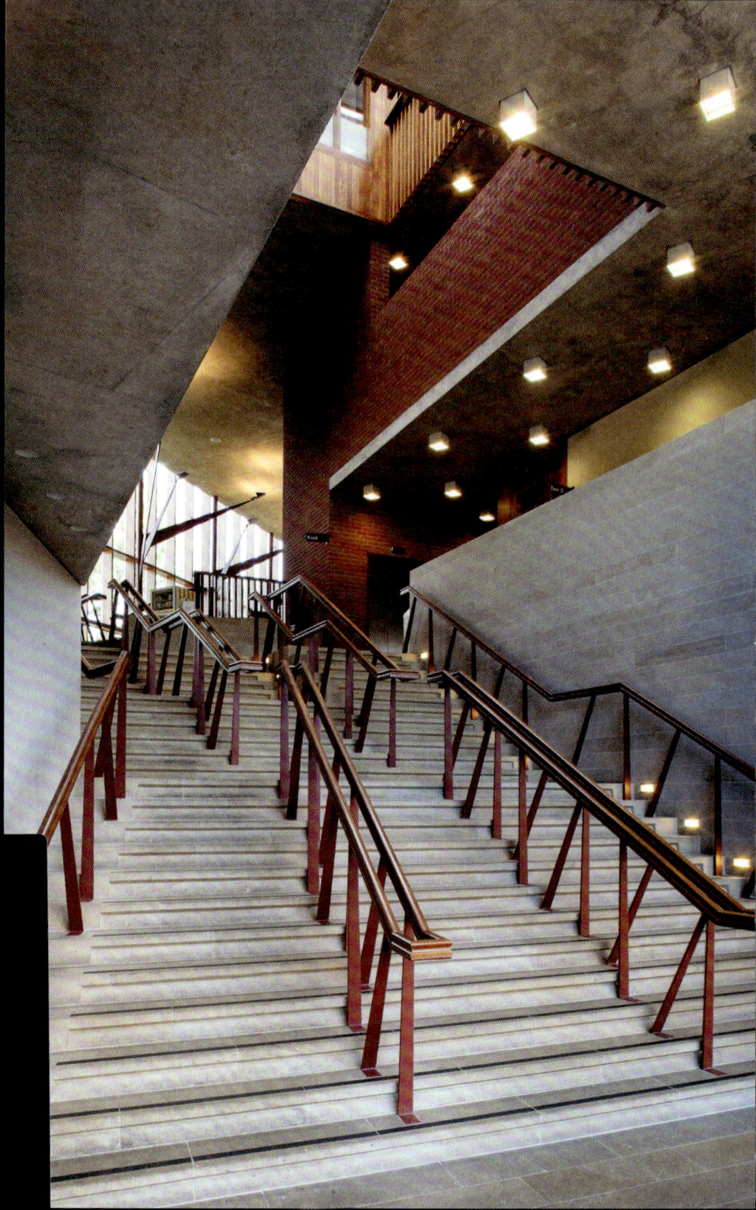

Lyric Theatre

Due to its leaky roof and resident rats, the old Lyric, built on the banks of the Lagan River, is hardly missed. The 1968 concrete building was razed in 2008 to make way for O'Donnell + Tuomey's structure. Shortlisted for the 2012 Stirling Prize, the new Lyric is a triumph, crafted out of iroko wood and 21 types of brick, a nod to Belfast's industrial heritage. Clever features include a glass-fronted rehearsal room that gives a glimpse of the actors at work; a skewed aisle in the 380-seat theatre that avoids the customary 'dead' central space; and natural light and ventilation throughout. The theatre staged plays throughout the Troubles and in 2012 was the host venue for the extraordinary handshake between the Queen and Sinn Féin minister Martin McGuinness.
55 Ridgeway Street, T 028 9038 1081, www.lyrictheatre.co.uk

Queen's University
Camouflaged behind trees on a residential road, the School of Planning, Architecture and Civil Engineering (above; Chlorine Gardens) was originally designed in the 1980s by architects Ferguson McIlveen. Recognising it needed a new lease of life, the university called on Todd Architects + Planners to clad the facade in compressed fibre panels manufactured by Netherlands-based Trespa Meteon. Inside, there was a major overhaul too. Beyond Gigacer's basaltina stone on the ground floor, there is birch-veneer panelling and screens, and natural light and ventilation. Despite it being in contrast to the Victorian streets of south Belfast, the building is somehow close to the area's verdant spirit. In 2005, Todd Architects also reclad the tired 1970s student union a few streets away.
www.qub.ac.uk

Linen Hall Library
Given that so many architectural gems are crumbling in the city centre, it's heartening to see this 18th-century library revived by architects Hall Black Douglas. Founded in a former linen warehouse in 1788, it holds more than a million books, including an outstanding collection of titles on Northern Irish politics. Scoot up to the first level from Donegall Square North to travel back in time: the floor resembles a Victorian gentlemen's club, featuring darkwood panelling, shelves in gentle disarray and a members' area lit by green banker lamps. A 2000 extension (above) links to an adjoining warehouse and connects to the main building via a four-storey staircase, the western wall made of glass. The result was a 50 per cent increase in space.
17 Donegall Square North,
T 028 9032 1707, www.linenhall.com

Fortwilliam Train Depot

Great plans are afoot for Belfast's transport system: a new £100m hub is due at Great Victoria Street Station and the Europa Buscentre, designed to handle 13 million passengers a year by 2030; and a new interchange mooted for the Cathedral Quarter's north-eastern edge. Keeping some of the rolling stock gleaming will be this train-cleaning shed, designed by RPP Architects and completed in 2005.

The 170m-long ribbed structure stables Translink NI Railways' high-tech Class 3000 trains, which ply the tracks to Bangor, Portadown and Derry-Londonderry. The closest you will get to the sleek building is by driving along the M2. Try to pass by at night, when the facility's curvilinear form, a 2008 Institution of Structural Engineers award-winner, is bathed in purple light.
www.robinsonpatterson.com

ARCHITOUR

078

Ulster Hall
Built by industrial bigwigs to entertain the city's growing working class, William Joseph Barre's 1862 performance venue was upgraded in 1903. The home of the Ulster Orchestra has staged a pro-Home Rule speech by Winston Churchill and appears in James Joyce's *Ulysses*. A 2009 restoration by Consarc and Tandem Design made space for other events.
34 Bedford Street, T 028 9033 4400

SHOPPING
THE BEST RETAIL THERAPY AND WHAT TO BUY

A taxi is the best way to access Belfast's most interesting retailers, which tend to be housed in workshops and by-appointment ateliers beyond the centre. Exceptions cluster around Wellington Street, home to craft shop Coppermoon (3 Wellington Street, T 028 9023 5325). Nearby is the reclaimed-furniture collective ReFound (7 Wellington Place, T 07811 342 444) and North Clothing (54 Howard Street, T 028 9050 7700), which offers made-to-measure Donegal tweed suits. Call into Lunn's (Queen's Arcade, T 028 9032 9799) for vintage Patek Philippe, Rolex and Breitling watches.

The gilet-and-big-shades drag that is Lisburn Road, a quick cab ride south-west, is the key suburban shopping spot. Although diminished from their pre-recession days, niche stores still thrive here. Pick up H&W Belfast Relish at 1933 delicatessen Arcadia (378 Lisburn Road, T 028 9038 1779) and head back to town via vintage emporium The Rusty Zip (28 Botanic Avenue, T 028 9024 9700). It's all a radical change from the bad old days. Between 1970 and 1975, bombs destroyed a quarter of the city centre's retail space, and department stores such as Robinson & Cleaver (see p051) went to the wall. One institution that survived it all is the 1896 St George's Market (12-20 East Bridge Street, T 028 9043 5704; Friday to Sunday), which does a roaring trade in Portavogie fish, veg and street fashion against a backdrop of live bands.
For full addresses, see Resources.

Derek Wilson Ceramics
Following his break at the RCA's Ceramic Art London show in 2010, Derek Wilson now exports his sculptural tableware to Japan, France, Switzerland and the US. The University of Ulster graduate, who cites Ben Nicholson and other modernists as inspirations, hand-throws porcelain bowls, water pitchers (above left), £260, and tumblers (above right), £70, bisque firing before finishing them with celadon glaze or engobe. The result is a series of elegant, idiosyncratic forms that span utility and ornamentation. Wilson's wheel is now spinning in a former mill in East Belfast, a focal point for artists as well as outlets such as The Bureau (see p085). He is currently looking into new glazes and techniques. Visits by appointment only.
B4 Portview, 310 Newtownards Road, www.derekwilsonceramics.com

Studio, Derek Wilson Ceramics

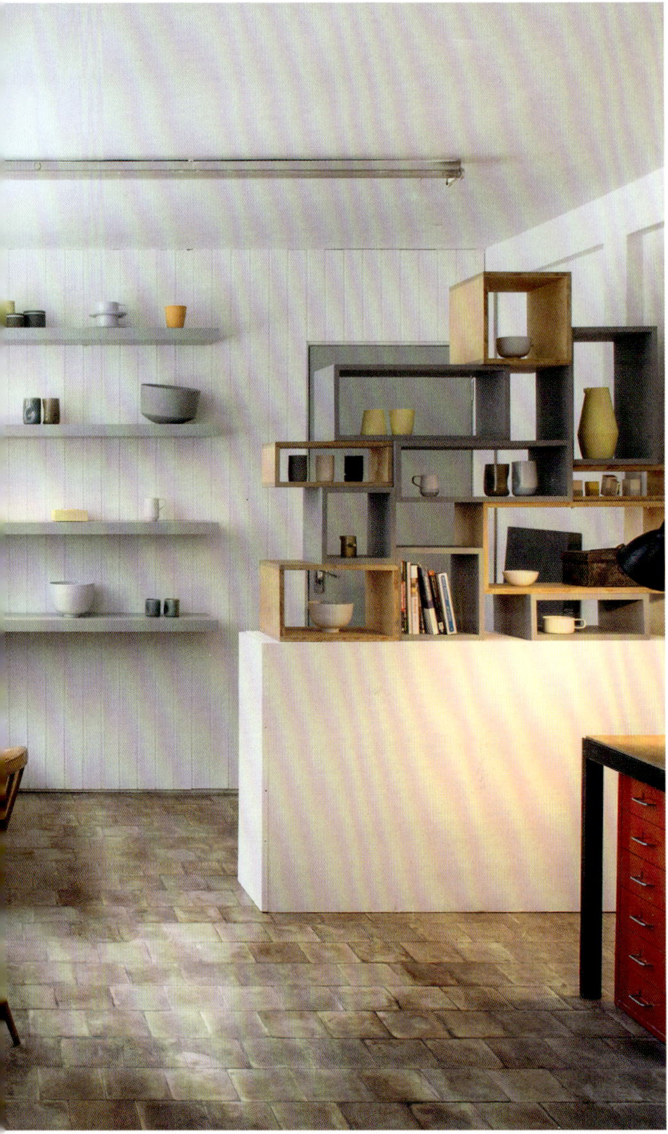

Envoy of Belfast
Selling Maria Rudman's reindeer-hide bracelets embroidered by Sami tribes, printed shirts from Paul Harnden and jewellery from Beirut's RosaMaria, Ruth Spence's 2007 boutique is a paean to witty, international womenswear. Spence regularly scours the world's fashion capitals for new lines and her travails have paid off with several exclusive deals. Film crews flying in to shoot in Belfast have now joined her loyal local clientele. Envoy's interior matches the high quality of the stock, featuring a battered seat salvaged from a Belfast tram, Paul Smith chairs and a central steel display table from the Tuscany-based manufacturer Heron Parigi. Cire Trudon candles lend an olfactory element to the space.
4 Wellington Street, T 028 9031 1110, www.envoyofbelfast.com

The Bureau

QCs, brickies and lawyers are among the fans of this men's emporium, founded by Michael Hamilton and Paul Craig in the city centre in 1989. Keen to explore a new web and showroom model, the duo relocated to East Belfast in 2012. The owner-designed interior, punctuated by blow-ups of Trojan Records album covers, and portraits (above) by the Belfast artist Paul Wilson, has no storeroom: customers are invited to hunt out the latest arrivals in the shop. The Bureau was chosen as Engineered Garments' first European stockist and sells Irish knitwear from Inis Meáin, Tricker's footwear, Orslow jeans, and raincoats by Ten C. A range of linen scarves and shirts carries The Bureau's own label, Merchants And Missionaries.
B2 Portview, 310 Newtownards Road, T 028 9046 0190, www.thebureaubelfast.com

Terry

When Obama, Cameron and other power brokers hunkered down *sans* aides at the 2013 G8 summit at Lough Erne, they gathered around a burr elm conference table made by this Portadown design studio. Founded by brothers Terry and Ross McDonagh in 2007, the brand is the latest realisation of the family furniture business, started by the siblings' carpenter grandfather in 1898. Eschewing mass production, the factory, located 30 minutes west of Belfast, produces one-off utilisations of reclaimed timber, steel, stone and glass. An 18-strong team works with architects and designers on projects such as Derry-Londonderry's barracks-turned-Turner Prize host gallery, private houses, shops, offices and restaurants.
169-173 Obins Street, Portadown, T 028 3833 3215, www.terrydesign.co.uk

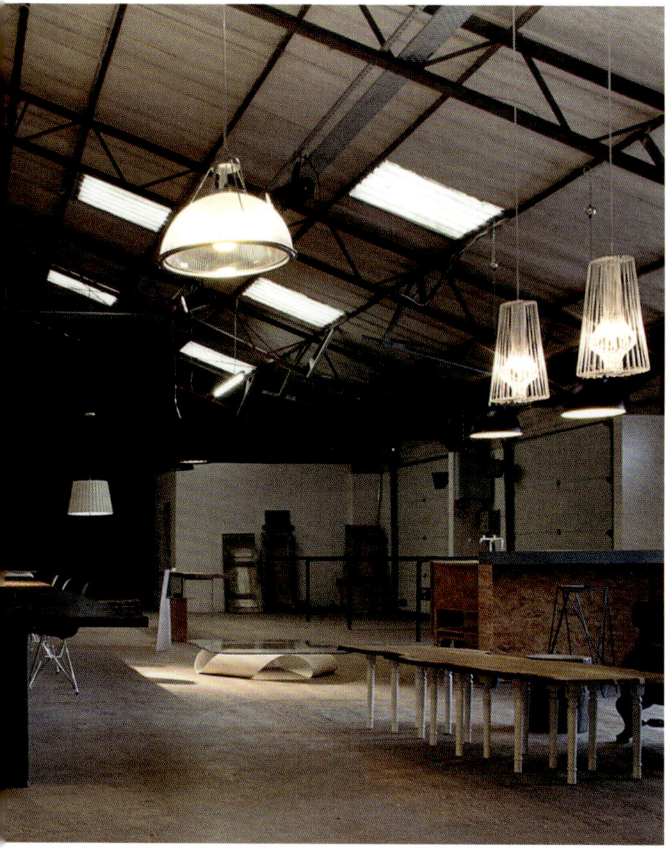

SPORTS AND SPAS
WORK OUT, CHILL OUT OR JUST WATCH

Forget the cold glint of air-conditioned gyms, Belfast's preferred pursuits take place in vast expanses of land and sea. The province boasts some 100 golf courses, with local Rory McIlroy rating Royal County Down (36 Golf Links Road, Newcastle, T 028 4372 3314) as one of the best. Sea legs develop early: children plastered in buoyancy aids sail across Belfast Lough from places such as Royal North of Ireland Yacht Club (7 Seafront Road, T 028 9042 8041).

Stormont legalised betting shops in 1957, three years before Westminster, placing horse racing close to the Ulsterman's heart. Twenty minutes south-west of town is Down Royal Racecourse (Maze, Lisburn, T 028 9262 1256), its refurbished pavilion and stands drawing thousands of punters. Investment is piling into the city faster than a camogie striker. The 11,000-capacity Odyssey Arena (2 Queens Quay, T 028 9073 9074) hosts Belfast Giants ice hockey face-offs, and Queen's University has ploughed £20m into its sports facilities in Botanic Park and Upper Malone Road (see p094). Not far from the latter is the upgraded athletics circuit, Mary Peters Track (Upper Malone Road, T 028 9060 2707).

Hamilton Architects' renovation of Ulster Rugby's Ravenhill ground (85 Ravenhill Park, T 028 9049 3222) is due in 2014. Projects set for 2015 include a £76m Gaelic football and hurling stadium at Casement Park (88-104 Andersonstown Road, T 028 9030 0172). *For full addresses, see Resources.*

The Spa at The Merchant Hotel

Giving you another reason not to set foot outside Belfast's leading hotel (see p020) for a few days is its in-house spa, opened in 2010. CM Design Consultants carved out a small but perfectly formed subterranean space comprising five treatment rooms, a sauna, steam room, hydro pool and an ice fountain; and offering treatments using Sodashi, Kerstin Florian and bee-venom products. The gloaming is leavened by bright furnishings: a white 'Bibendum' chair by Eileen Gray, a 'Wingback' sofa from Tom Dixon and artworks that are rotated on a regular basis. When your treatment has finished (we recommend the hot lava-shell massage), delay your return to the outside world with a glass of champagne in the crepuscular café.
16 Skipper Street, T 028 9026 2712, www.themerchanthotel.com

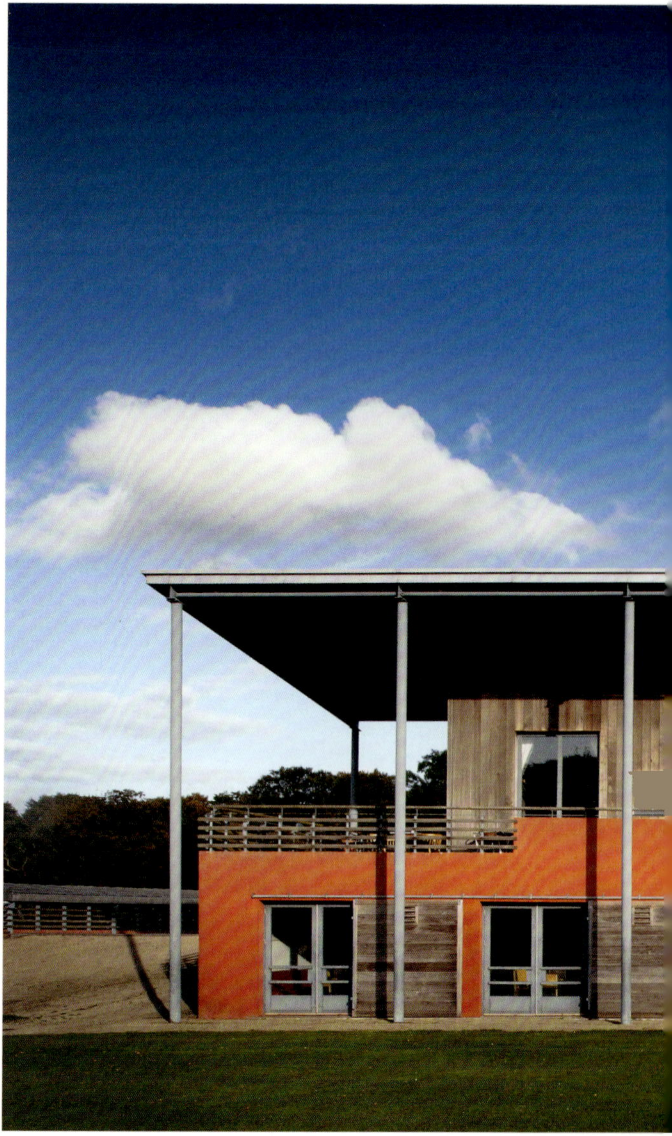

Blackwood Golf Centre

While star-in-the-making Rory McIlroy was thwacking prodigious 40-yard drives in Holywood in the early 1990s, this 1994 golf centre was being built down the road. O'Donnell + Tuomey have referenced the rural setting with farm-style buildings, constructed using cedarwood and steel, and a landscape-hugging car park. The bar/restaurant has a great view of the 18th hole. Twelve miles east of Belfast, Blackwood is rated as one of Northern Ireland's top 'pay and play' drives, offering both a par 71 championship course and a beginner-friendly par 3 option. Those lacking McIlroy's precision should head to the driving range, which has a practice bunker and automated ball delivery.
150 Crawfordsburn Road, Clandeboye, Bangor, T 028 9185 2706

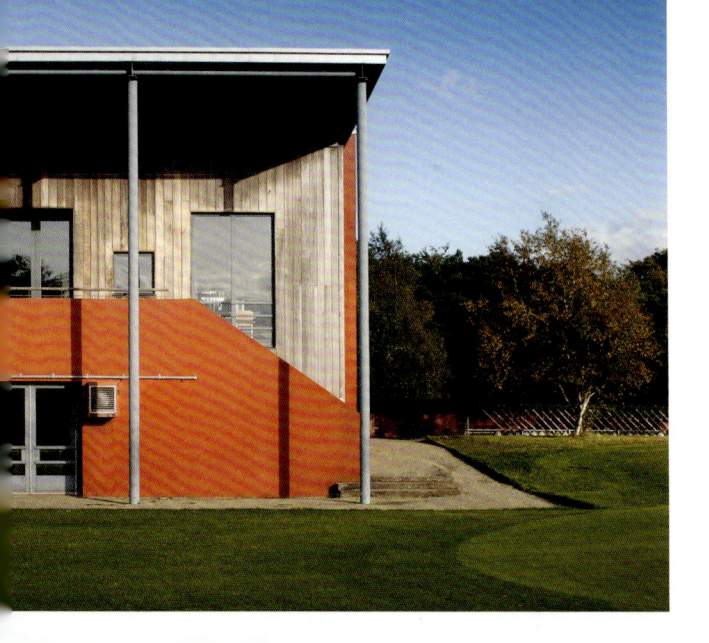

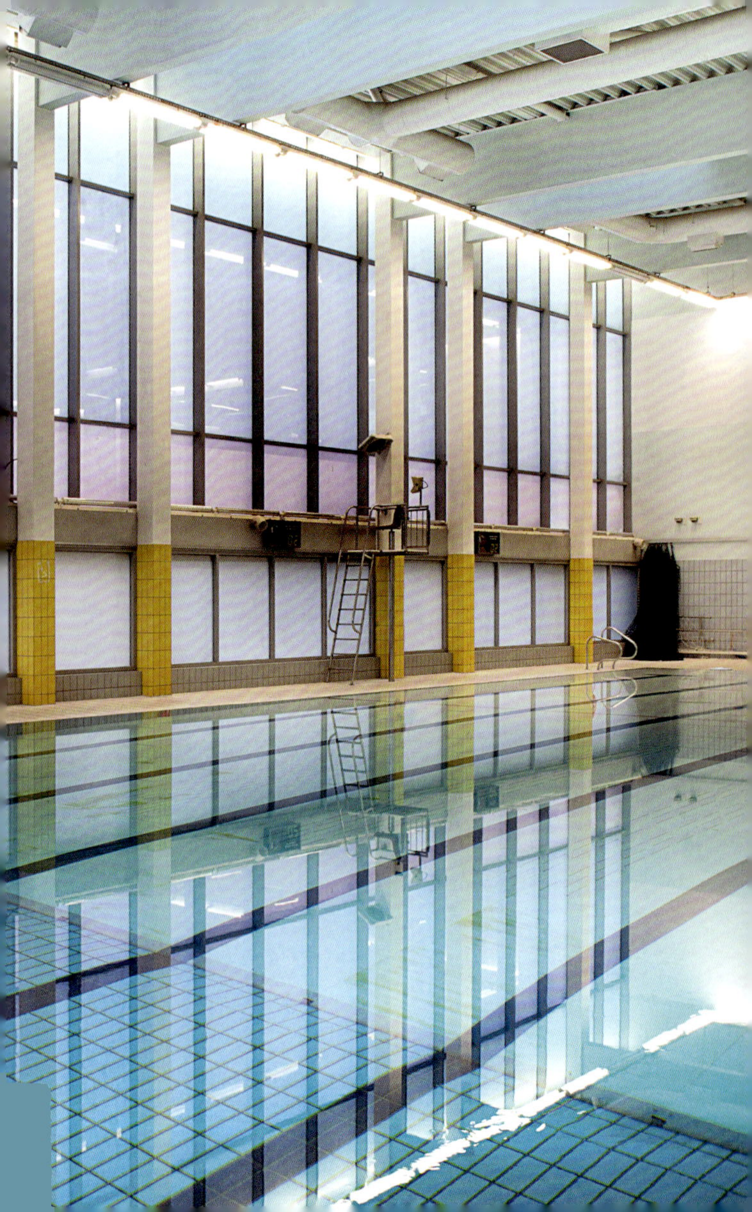

Falls Leisure Centre

A cuboid of translucent purple, blue and green, Kennedy FitzGerald & Associates' 2005 leisure centre stands out a mile on west Belfast's Falls Road. The £6.1m RIBA-award-winning building replaced a far more ordinary swimming complex, and was constructed to help revitalise one of the city's poorest districts. Eco features include natural ventilation and lighting. You can peer into the 25m swimming pool (opposite) from the street through Okalux glass panels; rays pour into the sports hall; and rainwater cleans the pool's filters. After dark, an intelligent control system fires up Zumtobel's energy-efficient lights, giving the structure an iridescent glow. The centre also houses a sauna, gym, exercise studios and a laser-game labyrinth.
15-17 Falls Road, T 028 9050 0510,
www.belfastcity.gov.uk

Queen's Sport Botanic PEC
Dating to 1971, Queen's sports centre has planted a 25m pool with a high-diving board into Botanic Park. FaulknerBrowns' £7m extension introduced a wood-clad rotunda with a translucent roof. Completed in 2006 and fitted out by Gilbert-Ash, the new space added an expansive entrance, a climbing wall and cave, gym and cycling studio to the mix. If the two sports halls, 10 squash courts, all-weather pitch and golf simulator (devised by the psychology faculty) don't tempt you, let the experts show you how it's done on the television screens in Clements Café. The university also spent £13m transforming its Upper Malone Road base (T 028 9062 3946), creating the UK and Ireland's only rugby, soccer and Gaelic games pitch.
Botanic Park, T 028 9068 1126, www.queenssport.com

SPORTS

ESCAPES

WHERE TO GO IF YOU WANT TO LEAVE TOWN

There is an upside to Belfast's scything road network: a sense of adventure will put you on traffic-free highways within minutes, leading to a dramatic coastline and country retreats. The theme is resolutely outdoors, but don't expect to return home with a tan; the province is renowned for its squalls interspersed with heavy showers. The de facto escape is two hours' drive west in County Donegal, situated in Ulster but, due to the meandering pen of 1921 partition cartographers, over the border in the Republic of Ireland. Belfast denizens go misty-eyed at the mention of this land of white sands (visit Portsalon or Rosapenna).

The most spectacular drive is north along the Antrim coast. The prize for conquering this road is the Giant's Causeway (see p098), then a nip at Old Bushmills' Distillery (2 Distillery Road, Bushmills, T 028 2073 3218). Serious imbibers can repair to The Bushmills Inn (9 Dunluce Road, Bushmills, T 028 2073 3000). To the south is the Ards Peninsula, whose big skies and clear light have made it a hotspot for creatives. Stay at the Portaferry Hotel (The Strand, Portaferry, T 028 4272 8231) and take a tour of the neoclassical Mount Stewart House (Portaferry Road, Newtownards, T 028 4278 8387). If you prefer admiring fine scenery from a fireside, follow the world's leaders to Lough Erne (Belleek Road, Enniskillen, T 028 6632 3230), a five-star hotel set in 98 sweeping hectares.

For full addresses, see Resources.

Slieve Donard Resort and Spa
Whereas the Europa (see p022) is Hastings' urban bolthole, this is the group's rural retreat. Located 30 miles south of Belfast, it was built as a grand hotel, complete with its own vegetable plots and pigs, by the Belfast and County Down Railway in 1898. Taking over in 1972, Hastings has maintained the upmarket standard with classy afternoon teas and packages in the spa (above). The Oak Restaurant serves a good local menu, while the clubby Percy French restaurant in the grounds offers more casual fare. It's a golfer's paradise too. The Royal County Down course (see p088) is steps away, and links at Ardglass, Kilkeel and Warrenpoint are nearby. Of the 178 rooms, reserve an Executive Double for uplifting views of the Irish Sea or Mournes. *Down Road, Newcastle, T 028 4372 1066, www.hastingshotels.com*

Giant's Causeway, County Antrim
You could blithely whizz by the Giant's Causeway — 40,000 hexagonal basalt columns (the apocryphal remains of a bridge built by giant Finn McCool in order to bash his Scottish rival, Fingal). Today, Heneghan Peng's Visitor Centre (above), a 2013 RIBA-award nominee, is a similarly covert beast: an £18.5m piece of 'land art' propped up by locally sourced basalt columns of its own and crouching under a grass-covered roof. Replacing a bog-standard building that burned down in 2000, the 1,800 sq m centre is managed by the National Trust, which claims it to be its most innovative facility. Ground-source pumps warm sea air to heat the structure, which houses an interactive exhibition, a café and a shop.
44 Causeway Road, Bushmills,
T 028 2073 1855, www.nationaltrust.org.uk

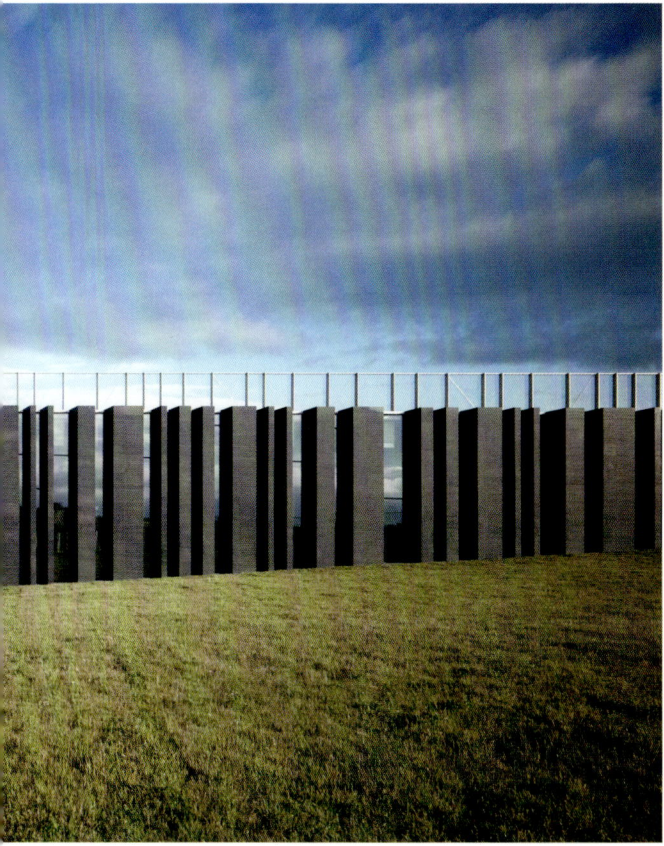

Regional Cultural Centre, Co Donegal
More space station than arts complex, MacGabhann Architects' cultural centre landed in Donegal in 2007, up the road from the 1999 An Grianán Theatre (T +353 749 120 777). The sharply angled building with windows rendered in aluminium and glass introduced a 150-seat performance space-cum-cinema, foyer galleries and digital media suites to the market town, known for its 1901 neo-Gothic St Eunan's Cathedral but often passed through en route to the northern beaches. Besides art shows, there's a programme boasting genuine international coups. The local community is engaged via strong social history initiatives, panel discussions and cross-border film screenings.
Port Road, Letterkenny, Republic of Ireland, T +353 749 129 186, www.regionalculturalcentre.com

101

ESCAPES

102

St Aengus' Church, County Donegal
Sublime rotundas run deep in these parts. Dating to 1,700BC, the ring fort of Grianán Áiligh stands proud on a hillside overlooking Lough Swilly in the parish of Burt, on the N13 Derry-Londonderry to Letterkenny road. More than 3,600 years later, this wonderful 1967 Roman Catholic church spiralled out of the heavy podzolic soil minutes down the hill. The architect, Donegal's Liam McCormick, was clearly inspired by the Bronze Age fortification, designing a circular structure rendered in stone and draped with a copper roof tapering via an oculus into a sharp spire. Open the heavy copper door to explore the spartan interior, whose most striking feature is Helen Moloney's vibrant stained glass. Tying fort and church together is Oisín Kelly's free-standing wall outside, sporting a series of circular forms.
Carrownamaddy, Burt, Republic of Ireland, T +353 287 126 2302

NOTES
SKETCHES AND MEMOS

RESOURCES
CITY GUIDE DIRECTORY

A
Aether & Echo 040
 11 Lower Garfield Street
 T 028 9023 9163
Arcadia 080
 378 Lisburn Road
 T 028 9038 1779
 www.arcadiadeli.co.uk

B
The Bar + Grill at James Street South 048
 21 James Street South
 T 028 9560 0700
 www.belfastbargrill.co.uk
Belfast Banking Company Building 064
 Donegall Street/Waring Street
Belfast Exposed 028
 The Exchange Place
 23 Donegall Street
 T 028 9023 0965
 www.belfastexposed.org
Berts 052
 The Merchant Hotel
 16 Skipper Street
 T 028 9026 2713
 www.themerchanthotel.com
Bittles Bar 040
 70 Upper Church Lane
Blackwood Golf Centre 090
 150 Crawfordsburn Road
 Clandeboye
 Bangor
 T 028 9185 2706
 www.blackwoodgolfcentre.com
Botanic Gardens 062
 College Park
 Botanic Avenue
 T 028 9031 4762

Bread and Banjo Bakery 062
 353 Ormeau Road
 T 07720 961 310
The Bureau 085
 B2 Portview
 310 Newtownards Road
 T 028 9046 0190
 www.thebureaubelfast.com

C
Cafe Mauds 044
 555 Lisburn Road
 T 028 9543 8486
 6 Slofield Park
 Newcastle
 T 028 9332 9988
 www.mauds.co.uk
Casement Park 088
 88-104 Andersonstown Road
 T 028 9030 0172
 www.antrimgaa.net
Catalyst Arts Gallery 026
 Ground floor
 5 College Court
 T 028 9031 3303
 www.catalystarts.org.uk
City Hall 014
 Donegall Square
 T 028 9027 0456
 www.belfastcity.gov.uk/cityhall
Le Coop 040
 38 Hill Street
 T 028 9545 8120
 www.madeinbelfastni.com
Coppermoon 080
 3 Wellington Street
 T 028 9023 5325
 www.coppermoon.co.uk

Coppi 055
St Anne's Square
T 028 9031 1959
www.coppi.co.uk
The Crown Liquor Saloon 036
46 Great Victoria Street
T 028 9024 3187
www.nicholsonspubs.co.uk

D
Deanes 054
36-40 Howard Street
T 028 9033 1134
www.michaeldeane.co.uk
Deanes at Queens 029
1 College Gardens
T 028 9038 2111
www.michaeldeane.co.uk
Deanes Deli Vin Cafe 054
44 Bedford Street
T 028 9024 8830
www.michaeldeane.co.uk
Derek Wilson Ceramics 081
B4 Portview
310 Newtownards Road
www.derekwilsonceramics.com
El Divino 058
Mays Meadow
T 028 9032 2000
www.eldivino-belfast.com
Divis Tower 012
Divis Street
Down Royal Racecourse 088
Maze
Lisburn
T 028 9262 1256
www.downroyal.com

Duke of York 040
7-11 Commercial Court
T 028 9024 1062
www.dukeofyorkbelfast.com

E
Envoy of Belfast 084
4 Wellington Street
T 028 9031 1110
www.envoyofbelfast.com

F
Falls Leisure Centre 092
15-17 Falls Road
T 028 9050 0510
www.belfastcity.gov.uk
Flow Studio 062
52a Hill Street
T 028 9023 1981
www.flowstudiobelfast.com
Fortwilliam Train Depot 076
Off Shore Road
www.robinsonpatterson.com

G
Giant's Causeway Visitor Centre 098
44 Causeway Road
Bushmills
County Antrim
T 028 2073 1855
www.nationaltrust.org.uk
Golden Thread Gallery 026
84-94 Great Patrick Street
T 028 9033 0920
www.goldenthreadgallery.co.uk
Grand Opera House 070
Great Victoria Street
T 028 9024 1919
www.goh.co.uk

Grapevine 062
5 Pottingers Entry
T 028 9023 8182
An Grianán Theatre 100
Port Road
Letterkenny
County Donegal
Republic of Ireland
T +353 749 120 777
www.angrianan.com

H
Hadskis 040
33 Donegall Street/Commercial Court
T 028 9032 5444
www.hadskis.co.uk
Home Restaurant 061
22 Wellington Place
T 028 9023 4946
www.homepopup.com
The Hudson Bar 062
10-14 Gresham Street
T 028 9023 2322

J
James Street South 048
21 James Street South
T 028 9043 4310
www.jamesstreetsouth.co.uk
The John Hewitt 040
51 Donegall Street
T 028 9023 3768
www.thejohnhewitt.com

K
Kelly's Cellars 040
30-32 Bank Street
T 028 9024 6058

L
Linen Hall Library 075
17 Donegall Square North
T 028 9032 1707
www.linenhall.com
Love & Death 046
10a Anne Street
T 028 9024 7222
www.loveanddeathinc.com
Lunn's 080
Queen's Arcade
T 028 9032 9799
www.lunns.com
Lyric Theatre 072
55 Ridgeway Street
T 028 9038 1081
www.lyrictheatre.co.uk

M
MAC 025
10 Exchange Street West
T 028 9023 5053
www.themaclive.com
Made in Belfast 041
23 Talbot Street
T 028 9024 4107
1-2 Wellington Buildings
Wellington Street
T 028 9024 6712
www.madeinbelfastni.com
Mary Peters Track 088
Upper Malone Road
T 028 9060 2707
www.athleticsni.org/mary-peters-track
Menagerie 062
130 University Street
T 028 9023 5678
www.menageriebar.tumblr.com

Mount Stewart House 096
Portaferry Road
Newtownards
T 028 4278 8387
Mourne Seafood Bar 045
34-36 Bank Street
T 028 9024 8544
www.mourneseafood.com
Muriel's Café Bar 060
12-14 Church Lane
T 028 9033 2445

N
The National Grande Café 042
62-68 High Street
T 028 9031 1130
North Clothing 080
54 Howard Street
T 028 9050 7700
www.northclothing.com

O
Odyssey Arena 088
2 Queens Quay
T 028 9073 9074
www.odysseyarena.com
Old Bushmills' Distillery 096
2 Distillery Road
Bushmills
T 028 2073 3218
www.bushmills.com
OX 038
1 Oxford Street
T 028 9031 4121
www.oxbelfast.com

P
Il Pirata 055
279-281 Upper Newtownards Road
T 028 9067 3421
The Potted Hen 050
Edward Street
T 028 9023 4554
www.thepottedhen.co.uk

Q
Queen's Sport Botanic PEC 094
Botanic Park
T 028 9068 1126
www.queenssport.com
Queen's Sport Upper Malone 094
Upper Malone Road
T 028 9062 3946
www.queenssport.com
Queen's University 030/074
University Road
T 028 9097 5252
www.qub.ac.uk

R
Ravenhill 088
85 Ravenhill Park
T 028 9049 3222
www.ulsterrugby.com
ReFound 080
7 Wellington Place
T 07811 342 444
www.refoundonline.com
Regional Cultural Centre 100
Port Road
Letterkenny
County Donegal
Republic of Ireland
T +353 749 129 186
www.regionalculturalcentre.com

Robinson & Cleaver Terrace 051
Donegall Square North
T 028 9031 2666
www.robinsonandcleaver.com

Robinson & Cleaver Urban Deli 051
Donegall Square North
T 028 9031 2538
www.robinsonandcleaver.com

The Royal County Down Golf Club 088
36 Golf Links Road
Newcastle
T 028 4372 3314
www.royalcountydown.org

Royal North of Ireland Yacht Club 088
7 Seafront Road
T 028 9042 8041
www.rniyc.org

The Rusty Zip 080
28 Botanic Avenue
T 028 9024 9700
www.therustyzip.com

S

St Aengus' Church 102
Carrownamaddy
Burt
County Donegal
Republic of Ireland
T +353 287 126 2302

St Anne's Cathedral 009
Donegall Street
www.belfastcathedral.org

St George's Market 080
12-20 East Bridge Street
T 028 9043 5704

Samson and Goliath 010
Queen's Island
www.harland-wolff.com

Satis House 026
86 Deramore Avenue
T 07921 072 309
www.satis-house.com

Sawers 062
Fountain Centre
College Street
T 028 9032 2021
www.sawersbelfast.com

Shu 056
253 Lisburn Road
T 028 9038 1655
www.shu-restaurant.com

Skainos Project 066
239 Newtownards Road
T 028 9073 8989
www.skainos.org

The Spa at The Merchant Hotel 089
The Merchant Hotel
16 Skipper Street
T 028 9026 2712
www.themerchanthotel.com

The Spaniard 062
3 Skipper Street
T 028 9023 2448
www.thespaniardbar.com

Stormont 009
Upper Newtownards Road
T 028 9052 1802
www.niassembly.gov.uk

Sunflower 062
65 Union Street
T 028 9023 2474
www.sunflowerbelfast.com

T
Templemore Swim & Fitness Centre
064
Templemore Avenue
T 028 9045 7540
www.templemorebaths.org.uk
Terry 086
169-173 Obins Street
Portadown
T 028 3833 3215
www.terrydesign.co.uk
Titanic Belfast 034
1 Olympic Way
Queen's Road
T 028 9076 6386
www.titanicbelfast.com
Titanic's Dock & Pump-House 031
Queen's Road
Queen's Island
T 028 9073 7813
www.titanicsdock.com

U
Ulster Hall 078
34 Bedford Street
T 028 9033 4400
www.ulsterhall.co.uk
Ulster Museum 065
Botanic Gardens
T 028 9044 0000
www.nmi.com/um

V
Victoria Square 068
1 Victoria Square
T 028 9032 2277
www.victoriasquare.com

W
Waterfront Hall 069
2 Lanyon Place
T 028 9033 4400
www.waterfront.co.uk

Y
Yellow Door 051
427 Lisburn Road
T 028 9038 1961
www.yellowdoordeli.co.uk

HOTELS
ADDRESSES AND ROOM RATES

The Bushmills Inn 096
Room rates:
double, £130
9 Dunluce Road
Bushmills
T 028 2073 3000
www.bushmillsinn.com

Culloden Estate and Spa 016
Room rates:
double, £165
Bangor Road
Holywood
T 028 9042 1066
www.hastingshotels.com

Europa 022
Room rates:
double, from £155;
Titanic Suite, from £515
Great Victoria Street
T 028 9027 1066
www.hastingshotels.com/europa-belfast

The Fitzwilliam Hotel 018
Room rates:
double, from £155;
Corner Deluxe, from £180
Great Victoria Street
T 028 9044 2080
www.fitzwilliamhotelbelfast.com

Lough Erne Resort 096
Room rates:
double, from £110
Belleek Road
Enniskillen
T 028 6632 3230
www.lougherneresort.com

Malmaison 017
Room rates:
double, from £120;
Goliath Suite, £320;
Samson Suite, £420
34-38 Victoria Street
T 0844 693 0650
www.malmaison.com

The Merchant Hotel 020
Room rates:
double, from £160;
Art Deco Deluxe, £180
16 Skipper Street
T 028 9023 4888
www.themerchanthotel.com

Park Avenue 016
Room rates:
double, £100
158 Holywood Road
T 028 9065 6520
www.parkavenuehotel.co.uk

Portaferry Hotel 096
Room rates:
double, £90
The Strand
Portaferry
T 028 4272 8231
www.portaferryhotel.com

Radisson Blu 016
Room rates:
double, £100
The Gasworks
3 Cromac Place
Ormeau Road
T 028 9043 4065
www.radissonblu.co.uk/hotel-belfast

Slieve Donard Resort and Spa 097
Room rates:
double, £140;
Executive Double, from £150
Down Road
Newcastle
T 028 4372 1066
www.hastingshotels.com
Ten Square 023
Room rates:
double, £105;
Linenhall Suite, £200
10 Donegall Square South
T 028 9024 1001
www.tensquare.co.uk

WALLPAPER* CITY GUIDES

Executive Editor
Rachael Moloney

Author
Jonathan Lee

Art Director
Loran Stosskopf
Art Editor
Eriko Shimazaki
Designer
Mayumi Hashimoto

Photography Editor
Elisa Merlo
Assistant Photography Editor
Nabil Butt

Chief Sub-Editor
Nick Mee
Sub-Editors
Farah Shafiq
Vicky McGinlay

Editorial Assistant
Rodrigo Márquez

Intern
Rebeca Plaza

Wallpaper* Group
Editor-in-Chief
Tony Chambers
Publishing Director
Gord Ray
Managing Editor
Oliver Adamson

Contributors
Peter Chester-Williams
Alastair Hall
Cathy Law
Gerard McGuickin
Gascia Ouzounian
Gary Potter

Wallpaper* ® is a registered trademark of IPC Media Limited

First published 2014

All prices are correct at the time of going to press, but are subject to change.

Printed in China

PHAIDON

Phaidon Press Limited
Regent's Wharf
All Saints Street
London N1 9PA

Phaidon Press Inc
180 Varick Street
New York, NY 10014

Phaidon® is a registered trademark of Phaidon Press Limited

www.phaidon.com

A CIP Catalogue record for this book is available from the British Library.

All rights reserved. No part of this publication may be reproduced, stored in a retrieval system or transmitted, in any form or by any means, electronic, mechanical, photocopying, recording or otherwise, without the prior permission of Phaidon Press.

© 2014 IPC Media Limited

ISBN 978 0 7148 6656 7

PHOTOGRAPHERS

David Lyons/Alamy
St Aengus' Church,
pp102-103

Marie-Louise Halpenny
Giant's Causeway Visitor
Centre, pp098-099

Aidan Monaghan
Belfast city view,
inside front cover
Samson and
Goliath, pp010-011
Divis Tower, p012
Newtownards Road
mural, p013
City Hall, pp014-015
Malmaison, p017
The Fitzwilliam
Hotel, pp018-019
The Merchant Hotel,
p020, p021
Europa, p022
Ten Square, p023
MAC, p025
Catalyst Arts
Gallery, pp026-027
Belfast Exposed, p028
Deanes at Queens, p029
Ashby Institute, p030
Titanic's Dock & Pump-
House, p031, pp032-033
Titanic Belfast, pp034-035
The Crown Liquor
Saloon, p036, p037

OX, pp038-039
Made in Belfast, p041
The National Grande
Café, pp042-043
Cafe Mauds, p044
Mourne Seafood Bar, p045
Love & Death, pp046-047
James Street South,
pp048-049
The Potted Hen, p050
Robinson & Cleaver, p051
Berts, pp052-053
Deanes, p054
Coppi, p055
Shu, pp056-057
El Divino, p058, p059
Muriel's Café Bar, p060
Home Restaurant, p061
Lyndsey McDougall, p063
Ulster Museum, p065
Skainos Project,
pp066-067
Victoria Square, p068
Waterfront Hall, p069
Grand Opera House,
pp070-071
Lyric Theatre, p072, p073
School of Planning,
Architecture and Civil
Engineering, p074
Linen Hall Library, p075
Fortwilliam Train
Depot, pp076-077
Ulster Hall, pp078-079
Derek Wilson Ceramics,
p081, pp082-083
Envoy of Belfast, p084

The Bureau, p085
Terry, pp086-087
The Spa at The Merchant
Hotel, p089
Blackwood Golf
Centre, pp090-091
Falls Leisure Centre, p092,
p093
Queen's Sport Botanic PEC,
pp094-095

Dennis Gilbert/View
Regional Cultural
Centre, pp100-101

BELFAST
A COLOUR-CODED GUIDE TO THE HOT 'HOODS

SHANKILL
Murals are the main attraction for visitors to this mainly Protestant part of the city

QUEEN'S QUARTER
Belfast's verdant southern district has architectural, cultural and retail highlights

CATHEDRAL QUARTER
It's all happening in this zone, replete with contemporary arts venues and buzzy bars

TITANIC QUARTER
Regeneration has paid due homage to the city's engineering heritage and iconic ship

FALLS
A commitment to Gaelic culture past and present pervades this mostly Catholic area

ORMEAU
This is a suburb on the rise, as evidenced by the redevelopment of its historic bakery

CITY CENTRE
An elegant concentration of the capital's 19th-century architecture, funded by industry

EAST BELFAST
Sectarian murals line the streets but the Skainos Project heralds an alternative future

For a full description of each neighbourhood, see the Introduction.
Featured venues are colour-coded, according to the district in which they are located.